The Dark Art of POLITICS

The Dark Art of POLITICS

Simon Carr

Of all the activities of idle men,
politics is the most exciting.

Niccolo Machiavelli

Hodder Moa Beckett

ISBN 1-86958-605-0

© 1997 Simon Carr

Published 1997 by Hodder Moa Beckett Publisher Limited
[a member of the Hodder Headline Group}
4 Whetu Place, Mairangi Bay, Auckland, New Zealand

Printed by APG, Australia
Designed and produced by Hodder Moa Beckett
Typest by TTS Jazz
Cover photos: New Zealand Picture Library and Fotopacific

All rights reserved. No part of this publication may be reproduced or transmitted
in any form or by any means, electronic or mechanical, including photocopying, recording, or any information storage and retrieval system, without permission in writing from the publisher.

Contents

Introduction

IF YOU hadn't been involved as a voter, the politics of the last twenty-five years would have been hilarious. For a generation, at every election, politicians have said one thing and done precisely the opposite – not something a bit different, or even very different, but the full about-face, 180°, two-fingers-to-you opposite of that which they had promised to do.

• Muldoon campaigns vigorously on a right-wing ticket. Over his nine years of power he loots the public coffers and spends like a wild-eyed socialist.

• When Muldoon is used up, the working-class party Labour gets elected. They proceed like speed-crazed Thatcherites. To the electorate's credit, they re-elect the party to finish the job they started – immediately they stop doing it.

• Bolger sweeps to power promising 'the decent society' and to abolish the surcharge. At once, his government slashes benefits and actually increases the taxes on the old.

- Winston campaigns on a ticket of getting rid of "an evil National government", and is voted the balance of power. Instinctively he secures that party in government.

There are doubtless politicians who represent the Noble Art of Politics. But that book is being written by someone else; this book is about the rest of them.

1

Why do they do it?

WHEN a marketing whizz rumoured to be making three million dollars a year came round for a drink he expressed an interest in politics. Murray's a highly moral Christian businessman who writes cheques for water wells in India; he's concerned about the leadership of the country, he's worried about the general lack of integrity in the establishment, he wants to put something back into the community. So I looked for the most succinct way to explain to him what politics can be like, and settled comfortably on the Second Law of Darkness:

"When you want to damage someone," I said, "you know you are best to set yourself up in a friendly stance before attacking them, because friends inflict deeper wounds than enemies."

From the look on his face this was such a hit-in-one I didn't need to tell him the rest of it: "Your reputation will depend in large part on people being scared of you. Your friends will quickly decay into colleagues. And if you are successful, there will be no colleague you can trust. You will achieve nothing. Your career will end in failure. You'll be thrown out and no-one will miss you."

At this point, Richard Prebble would say, "Okay. But what about the downside?" (You have to have a certain temperament to make a joke like that.)

We don't normally think about political lives, any more than we really think about the weather. They aren't things we can affect. There they are and that's the end of it.

But politicians are anything but irrelevant. They profoundly influence the economy, the social services, the administration of justice. So when we step back and ask what is it that individual politicians are actually for, the question comes into focus.

What's the point of Don McKinnon?, for instance, is a question that has no obvious answer. Here is a man blessed with an ambassadorial mien and calming influence on those around him; he raises the tone of many local meetings. But it's hardly worth wondering in what way the country would have been worse off if Don McKinnon had never been elected to Parliament.

And the further we go down the list of national names the less answerable these questions become. Simon Upton has been in politics all his adult life; can he be said to have achieved anything? Paul East, intelligent, articulate, excellent company, has consistently (and a little mysteriously) maintained one of the highest positions in cabinet – would his c.v. get a job that would fulfil his potential? Jonathan Hunt, the longest-serving member, the father of Parliament, said his greatest achievement was introducing personalised car registration plates to New Zealand (something he may or may not have actually done).

But these are figures we all know something of. Upton's

short, East's urbane, Hunt is fat. When you go further down the batting order of this Parliament you'll find evidence of people you know nothing about at all. If we wanted to know what the point of Damien O'Connor was or Jill Peck or Bob Brownlee, or Mark White, or Gerry Simcock we wouldn't know where to start. Even now, after a year, we glimpse a name in a political story and think – "That's a familiar name, who are *they*?" There is an exception to this rule, and that's when the name is Larry Sutherland. In his tenth year as a parliamentarian here is the MP that even other MPs don't know about. I'd been looking for anonymous MPs for some months before registering him – your eye just skates over his name in all the lists he appears in. And he almost did something; he was the one who nearly left with Jim Anderton but, in the end, didn't.*

But in the scheme of things, these people are relatively prominent nonentities, because there is a whole raft of people who only come to light in some perk-busting campaign – names like Ronald Bailey, Gordon Christie, Leo Schultz and Bruce Barclay who served three terms as parliamentarians. They were never heard of before, never heard of since, and according to contemporaneous reports, never heard of at the time.

So when you see them from a distance you do have to ask the question then: what would the net effect of Bob and Rob, of Jack and Jill, of Arthur and Martha not having been in Parliament?

Considering their position, their pay and the prestige they expect (all of which are considerable) these people have careers of monstrous insignificance. They pass laws and regulations that most of us will never hear of and never be aware whether we're breaking or obeying them.

* NB: When considering examples of pointless politicians, the researchers neglected (significantly perhaps) to include the example of John Falloon

It is genuinely odd, isn't it? Unless you actively wanted to make a career of insignificance, to do nothing of value, to be held in the lowest of esteem, why would you fight like fury to get into Parliament? Because it is always hard, it is very hard to get into Parliament. And having got in it's even harder to get on.

In politics, your colleagues do not collaborate to promote you; they do not conspire for your success. They don't gather at the bar to devise ways of getting your profile up in the media. Everyone's a competitor and success only comes at the expense of your colleagues. All friendship in politics has a strain of melancholy, like lovely summer days in England: you know you can't rely on them.

Politics is not like business. The accounting periods are different. In business there are monthly board meetings where the financial officers report. Businesses constantly monitor whether they're making enough money to survive. In politics there is one accounting every three years. In between, a government can run up debts that would break a country (and because they can, they do).

In the absence of any real objective measure of success, politics is a very tender occupation. Mood, wit, panache, sentiment – these qualities of appearance, of promise and potential – are given more importance than in any other occupation (except, possibly, that adopted by serial wives).

Particularly outside cabinet, promise and potential are all that anyone really has. Thus, you can see politicians at close quarters exalted to the heights by an opinion poll and the next instant crashed to the depths by the promotion of an enemy.

And this mood thing extends to the media. They get sucked into the world they report on. They become part of the general hormone-stress. We remember the hysteria in their treatment of Bolger, how they turned on him after his first "decent society" election and ran him ragged (he couldn't get a word in edgeways for two years). They did the same to Winston after he signed up with National (Helen Clark had been confidently cast as the prime minister-in-waiting) – and the reaction to his superannuation proposal was rabid.

Similarly, when the Winebox judgment came out, the deceived journalists turned on Winston with a ferocity that surprised even him.

In all the maelstrom, Birch has almost necessarily come back into favour. His role is the Mr Stability while Winston and his party and his followers rollock around the decks. Birch is therefore able to run a six-month recession and a ten per cent devaluation without the media really remarking on it. We begin to see the actual merits of these individuals are wholly secondary to their mood merits.

Sharon Crosbie's mumsie observation about Parliament resembling a group of overtired toddlers doesn't catch half the complexity of what is happening. It's true that in the grand coalition of politicians and media, the Law of the Playground prevails – but it's a far more mature age group than toddlers we're talking about; these are intensely communicative creatures who deal in the intricate ebb and flow of jealousy, envy, malice, guilt, hero-worship and crude affection that constitutes the life of the playground. It starts around eight years old and never finishes.

As in any playground, certain things are irresistible. A fight will always have an audience. Punishment, especially severe, will inspire an awesome thrill over the whole school population. And someone losing their temper will be relished by everyone. This is why we, at primary school, used to pursue loose-tempered boys going "*Woo* bait! *Woo* bait! *Woobait woobait woobait!*"

Affectation is particularly punished. Walking like a film star in my day was immediately recognisable by the roll of the shoulders and holding the elbows a little out from the body, and any imitation of a hero's walk would draw a small crowd of observers: "*Look, he thinks he's a film star*!"

And now, *plus ça change*, we are still doing it – Tuku, Winston, Alamein, Robyn, Jenny, Jim . . . Affectation is remorselessly persecuted, apologies are viciously demanded and infuriatingly withheld; you rag an individual until the mood swings back in their favour; then you make up manfully in preparation for the next time your gang feels energetic enough to gang up on their gang.

These are basic social facts in western cultures; they start early and endure.

But let's go back to the beginning. What is it that drives politicians? One school of thought suggests that the very desire to become a politician should disqualify you from office: wanting to boss people around and have everyone listen to you is a character flaw so profound as to be self-defeating. This is a point well understood by politicians – they conceal their real motives so successfully that sometimes even they don't know why they are acting as they are. Ambition is a form of disloyalty, as Shakespeare's Mark Antony used to large effect in his famous speech over Caesar's body:

But Brutus says he was ambitious,
(and so they had to go and kill him, the bastards).

The thing that makes politicians work is a cold and rather frightening thing. But then, much of the world is driven by cold and impersonal forces.

For instance, it wasn't until I got a job in advertising that I realised advertisements weren't made purely to entertain you.

Worse, my new creative director didn't seem to admire the government-funded spots I'd written for the Ministry of Transport (you may remember it even now, twenty years later: "In thirty seconds, this girl's life will never be the same . . . " it began).

He didn't share the general enthusiasm, my new creative director from England (don't you hate these overseas experts?). "Forget the awards it won," he said, "that wasn't advertising, it was public relations. Advertising is about selling packaged goods. Now, here, this piece you have written is a piece of public relations for breadmakers. I want an advertisement for *this loaf of bread* as opposed to *that loaf of bread*" (both identical).

It was an experience of ulterior purpose that was shocking to a young idealist. It was like finding your close friends only laugh at your jokes because they like your sister; or that your grand passion, the love of your life, is only after your money.

Ten years later there was more shocking news. When we had launched the *Independent* in London our financial director broke it to me what companies were for. I had thought companies made things – washing machines, newspapers, amphibious cars. But no, companies only make one thing – a profit for the shareholders. The product is, as it were, a by-product. The shareholders of Newspaper Publishing plc were not in the game to create a new national daily newspaper; they had no interest in newspapers any more than in the toiletries, pharmaceuticals or copper mines they might otherwise be investing in. Had I been taught Adam Smith earlier in life I would have been less damaged by this drop in temperature and the sudden loss of spirits it caused.

And if you think things can't get any worse it's just a failure of the imagination because the next decade (in middle age already) I was shocked on a far larger scale reading the *Selfish Gene*, a book about evolutionary biology. Human beings, the assumption had been, were here to struggle, make love, and search for liberty and happiness. But according to evolutionary biology our search for knowledge, God and pure consciousness is just by-product. According to the operation of our DNA (the ancient replicators which form the basis of all life), human beings are merely giant, lumbering robots whose only purpose is to protect the genes they inherited and shepherd them on to another robot in the next generation.

And now I know, late in life, in the same cold way, politicians don't exist to provide security for the disabled or the unfortunate, they aren't in business either to create a welfare state or to get better value for money for taxpayer funds, not to privatise or nationalise state institutions; no, not even to try to improve the financial administration of the health and education systems. The purpose of politicians is to get their fingers into the sockets of power, and get that rush of meaning, reassurance and pleasure that makes them feel most alive.

Politicians rather dispute this, especially the nice ones. When cornered they argue that the power thing only applies to politicians on the dark side. There is, after all, a Noble Art theory of politics put about by Aristotle and others (Lockwood Smith, for one) which sees politics as the highest form of public service and politicians as honest professionals working tirelessly for the public good; cruelly misunderstood by a misguided public and a malevolent media ("Good news is no news, you see," they say sadly). Politics, they insist, has the same proportion of rogues as accountants and pharmacists. They argue they are no different from any other professional group – a little less generously paid perhaps for the hours they put in (oh, the hours are very demanding). What they say may even be true, in a certain light, but essentially it's piffle.

The view of this book is that darkness and deception, manipulation and machination and ulterior purpose are part of the natural condition, the normal operating procedures of politics. There are many expressions of this, but none greater than the example of Robert Muldoon, the Master of Darkness in our time. The latter part of his political career consisted of a complicated chiaroscuro of darkness laid upon the dark.

• He ignored the Gleneagles agreement he had signed with the Commonwealth to allow the Springboks to tour New Zealand. The resulting civil disturbances split the country in half like an apple and reached the proportions of a minor civil war – but it did mobilise the support of the khaki generation and resulted in Muldoon's final re-election (with a minority of the vote).

• He compiled and published a list of what he called public enemies and read it out on television (Donna Awatere, as she was then, led the list – but only because it was in alphabetical order, she modestly says).

• He organised a currency crisis for the incoming Labour government *after* his election defeat by continuing to act as the finance minister for the two weeks he was legally entitled to. Paradoxically, the crisis gave Labour the impetus to scrap Muldoon's panoply of state power.

• No-one knows the extent of his involvement in the events following the Air New Zealand crash at Erebus.

• He awarded himself a knighthood, fearing the incoming prime minister wouldn't do the traditional thing.

But everywhere we look we see darkness great and small:

David Lange ankle-tapped Mike Moore just before the 1993 election by going public with the need for tax hikes.

Michael Laws appeared tearfully on television to say that he was resigning from Parliament on a matter of honour (actually, misleading the House).

Jim Anderton resigned from the bruising hurly-burly of Parliament to "look after his family". He returned to the bruising hurly-burly to unseat Sandra Lee, while his family problems multiplied.

It's hardly fair to put in Alamein Kopu among these heavyweights but she did display glimpses of dark ability in and around her debacle. She signed a pledge promising to stay in the Alliance and then broke it; she told the media she was leaving the party before telling her colleagues; and said she'd rather be at Mat Rata's sick bed than in Parliament (the only thing that might have raised him from his bed in indignation).

Neil Kirton is done like a dinner by a National party that has no intention of abiding by the health policy in the coalition document. *And* the hand on the knife is Winston's.

The only pure example of a politician achieving without any practice of the dark art has been Ruth Richardson. From the moment she arrived in caucus to her rejection of the justice portfolio and resignation from Parliament, no-one was in any doubt about her objectives or her strategies for achieving them. Which is why she's not there any more, of course.

Even Roger Douglas, whose vision of public policy is so comprehensive, and coherent, and who had so much of the light that his ministerial office looked like a banker's rather than a politician's – even he had enough acquaintance with the dark art to push his enormous packages through the system.

At the fundamental level, there's very little to choose between politicians because they are fundamentally the same as each other, and fundamentally different from us. We'll develop this idea later on, but the first time they start making themselves available to us voters is when they start doing things.

Eighty per cent of parliamentarians cleverly don't do anything at all. They can be described as mainstream flotsam, seat-warmers, or (unkindly) trough-artists whose only function is to support the active twenty per cent. These 80-20 sets of parliamentarians are as different in kind as hammerheads and basking sharks, as heavyweights among shadow boxers, as SWAT squads from community police persons.

But the active fifth do engage in the great struggle, the policy battle (which is different from the political battle). This is the great struggle of the late twentieth century – and consists of two sharply divided tribes who argue for more government or less government, higher state spending or lower state spending, more taxes or lower taxes.

As the flower is to its DNA so policy programmes are to the power-seekers. With politics though, the DNA can produce widely (even wildly) different flowers, depending on how the environment changes.

The policy programmes are what draws out the politicians' will to power. They are important because that's what we voters can see and what we vote for. And in fairness, Richard Prebble, who knows something of the dark arts, also says: "If you haven't got the light as well as the dark you end up like Winston. Or like the darkest of them all, Michael Laws."

So at one extreme, if you let the dark arts overwhelm you it will be your destruction; your career will end like the last act of some Shakespearian history play, in a final, desperate conflict where the pious, godfearing man of justice comes in at the end and chops your head off. But, then again, you have to dabble in darkness at least, because if you don't have a mastery of the dark arts you will never triumph. If you don't have an acquaintance with them you won't achieve anything at all.

The confusing thing about modern power is that it's gone underground. The highly effective political correctness movement has worked to subvert the old white male authority structures, and now, to confess to an appetite for power is akin to an appetite for pornography. You just can't get away with it in respectable society. In fact, the complete opposite is the only line to take.

We saw a fine example of this in the privileges committee hearing which was testing the position of a list MP who left her party to go independent. Alamein Kopu and Sandra Lee struggled for supremacy by competing for the victim role. "I was abused," says one; "I thought she was going to hit me," says the other. "She shouted at me," and "She was rude to me," were all code words for, "She was trying to exercise power over me," the ultimate, unanswerable charge. (Imagine, even ten years ago in pre-PC days, Muldoon and Prebble talking like this: *"Robert's just been rude to me!"* – *"Richard's just raised his voice at me!"* That's how much society has changed in just a decade.)

Maybe this is why power is shared so much more today; it is required that we share what authority we have, we expect the performance of everyone we work with to be reviewed and appraised. It happens all through society. Bosses used to boss, now they consult and conciliate. Airline pilots who used to be supreme commanders of the flight deck now have their commands go round their navigator, first officer and co-pilot in a loop of approval; sergeant-majors used to frighten their men into obedience ("*Swagger!*" they used to shriek) – these days they consult; teachers used to instruct, often with the aid of some painful instrument – now they facilitate. The architecture of court rooms has changed from a gothic expression of awful authority to a community facility; Monarchs ride bicycles; multimillion-dollar entertainers wear jeans. And while ambitious and successful women are still power-dressing in their legal offices, traders and entrepreneurs are increasingly sitting tieless in cafes doing business on their cell phones.

This mateyness in politics is also confusing (it's a trick they play because it works). It disguises the cold fundamentals, the shocking realities, but as business is about profit, so politics is about the search for, the acquisition, the maintenance of power.

A number of factors conceal this machinery.

The sober, bourgeois business suits, the private language of public policy, the ordinary origins, the shared responsibility – all these create the illusion of a humdrum profession of mandarin administration. Thoroughly decent politicians like Wyatt Creech, Lockwood Smith, Phil Goff with their quiet professional activities – the consulting and the consensualising, the strategies for medium-term, they are all aspiring to the tranquillising effect of Bill Birch.

And the speed at which things happen helps their argument. The pace of implementing policy (or doing things, as we call it) has slowed so much that it's hard to see if anything's happening at all. In Roger Douglas' first ten months he had turned the entire economy upside-down. Here and now it takes a year to construct a regulatory framework to keep electricity price increases below the 5.9 per cent they are threatening. Ministers have been working for five years to decide who owns the telephone numbers we have (this is significant because if we the consumers own them we can switch between the phone companies day by day, for the better prices). Still there is no decision forthcoming.

There's very little actual fighting and what there is is more like televised pro-wrestling than street fighting, with its knives, tyre irons and sharpened car keys. Real conflict erupts only occasionally; usually the parties lean against each other like sumo wrestlers too tired to wrestle each other out of the ring.

So unlikely are we to see politicians damaged on parliamentary TV it doesn't occur to us that it's possible to hurt them any more. Sprightly Jack Elder goes to a meeting and his failure to get more police on the beat is ascribed to the fact that he is a "boy sent to do a man's job". It doesn't occur to us that this will distress him or keep him awake with feelings of anger and humiliation as a normal person would. "Prick us and do we not bleed?" a politician might ask and they'd have to conclude, "As a matter of fact we don't, really, no."

We've been conditioned by their calluses. We've seen Muldoon hanging on, we've seen Winston emerging from annihilating attacks, we've seen Bolger surviving in a furnace. Even Anderton's momentary absence on compassionate leave only strengthens the impression that these people are so battle-hardened as to be impenetrable.

But none of this is apparent when you have dinner in Bellamy's. They have disguised themselves in Hallenstein suits. But they are politicians. They have become different. The pain they can withstand is just the first of their unusual qualities.

Nearly everything they do, if they're any good, has an ulterior purpose; or at least, an extended purpose. For all their efforts to drink a bottle of beer like the rest of us, they have gone into this new, dangerous space. They can never have a normal conversation again. They will never say, "That's interesting, tell me more about that." Now they are the living example of the rule *the opposite of talking isn't listening: it's waiting*. They will never be able to apologise freely. They will never be able to sit unselfconsciously at a social function while someone else is the centre of attention. Their only deep refreshment comes from power, or from the radiant energy that comes off the powerful.

But because it's hard to spot this in Bellamy's, let us try a thought experiment. Let us imagine our parliamentarians in some period costume; picture them in some ancient, intricate building – one with long corridors, public meeting rooms and secret passages. Put them in a building where plots are naturally pursued, where stratagems, blackmails, threats are encouraged by the twisting passages and half-lit ante-rooms, a building where enormous bribes may be offered, like dukedoms with land and rents. There is a deep courtyard with a gallows and an execution block to remind us of the consequences of failure.

Then introduce into this Byzantine setting, gorgeous in his gilt-braided waistcoast and sheer black hose, Roger Sowry carrying his staff of office – we can tell how important he is by the size of his retinue which consists of scribes, counsellors, jesters, physicians, poisoners, valets and sedan-carriers. Follow him down a long corridor, past sudden alcoves where small groups whisper and darkly laugh, follow as he takes us into the great hall where the costly tapestries hang and where counsellors sit on their baronial thrones.

Here in a sumptuous purple dress high at the back, and dashed with emerald thread, the woman we know as Jenny Shipley, a sardonic smile concealed behind one of her heavily jewelled forefingers, she sits on her seat of power, saying little, but vigilant, and waiting, but for what?

Surely not for this large, hearty individual, a George I sort of character full of good spirits but with an imperfect grasp of English. Those who laugh behind his broad Bolgerian back are careful to rearrange their features before he turns to them. And for all their smirking, the fact is he has the largest train of all. He has counsellors, ambassadors, ministers, clerks, researchers, grammarians, astrologers, lexicographers, dancing masters, agriculturalists, sycophants, dressers, bankers, two torturers and a conversation coach.

But for all his size he is always moving, always on the move. He knows there is no easy return to the world, except through the courtyard with the gallows and the block.

He embraces, for reasons that aren't immediately apparent, an Othello. This one is glamorous, fascinating, swarthy, more opulently dressed than any of the others, and he sports a noble disdain for domestic hours. And his fabulous retinue sports a menagerie of exotics – Nubians, dwarves, warriors – unused to (and undressed for) this formal venue. He has a Fool. And he also has a Iago, but he is momentarily out of favour, dressed in black by the door, but Iago has also detained one of Othello's irascible lieutenants and is spinning his hypnotic influence over him . . .

What are they all doing here? Among all the intrigue, the detail, the common coin of the state's administration, the shared favours, the monopolies that are being distributed, the positions of influence brokered and bartered, they are all waiting, every one of them, for the King to falter.

They have been saying for five years now he's for the chop but no-one has offered to try and take him through the door into the awful courtyard. So he still walks the halls, and the sardonic smile behind the jewelled forefinger is getting tauter . . .

Outside the Palace a rabble of Puritans, peasant leaders, revolutionaries, aldermen, civic dignatories, town criers, and other riff-raff. Far away, almost out of reach of all the hurly-burly, a long-suffering plenty of taxpayers whose earnings fund all the glamour, colour and excitement in and around the Palace.

This is the setting for politics as it has always been: the Medicis, the Sultans, the Russian court. The business of these creatures is power. We can easily believe this now. The jealousies, the struggles, the plots and bribes. Status is precisely determined by the size of each one's retinue, their transports, their apartments in the Palace. They are totally absorbed in the game.

They may have once believed that they are there to put something back into the community, but that was before they looked over the edge, into the abyss – and before the abyss looked back.

In the hierarchy of things politicians will never admit to as a driving force, power is the first. There are two others, even less to their credit.

No politician will admit in public to the pursuit of power as their driving force. No leader will ever say: "Vote us power!"
1 They say, "Let's work together to get rid of this hard-hearted, mean-spirited government and by giving a voice to the unheard masses we can put some *compassion* and commonsense back into public life." Hard-heartedness is becoming stale through overuse, and unethical behaviour is now a favoured line of attack: "Let's get rid of this sleazy government with their underwear bills and stamp warrants and brother-in-law contracts, and get some *integrity* back into the system."

The juniors, of course, don't have to defend themselves from charges of power-mania because they haven't got any power. They can laugh it off ("Power? A chance would be a fine thing") because they know in the grand scheme of things they are largely pointless. However, they *can* organise meetings with a furtive bureaucracy for their constituents, they can recommend names for state largesse in boards, tribunals, quangoes, and commissions, and once in a lifetime (or in Labour's case three times in a year) they can support new emerging leaders to threaten the hierarchy.

And if this doesn't add up to power it amounts to recognition, which is the appearance of power.

And they are also rewarded with aids to self-importance, which can be a very acceptable substitute. They are given parliamentary questions to ask of the seniors in the House. A challenging parliamentary question sounds like: "Can the minister confirm that owing to the government's prudent management the economy has entered a period of strong growth with many employment benefits?"

That a sense of power dresses these office-holders with an aura of glamour is proven when you see them after the office has been given to someone else.

A great admirer of Ruth Richardson noted that when he used to go and see her as a minister he'd spend a morning preparing for a twenty-minute meeting so as to get as many points across to her in the time available – and there was never enough time to discuss everything they wanted to. By contrast, when she came to see him after she had lost office he noticed himself glancing at his watch after ten minutes and thinking how much work he had to do. The point of her – the power she had – was no longer a part of the package.

And Ruth was one of the entities of government. She was one of the rare ones. So what must become of Mike Moore after he loses his seat? He goes to live on a mud dredger – what's the point of him then? Jim Bolger – unless he wins the republican debate and becomes our first President – he'll be reduced to sitting on the board of a savings company, or helping some industry group lobby: no commercial job is like the prime minister's. How could he ever recapture the glamour of office in civilian life?

2 The second thing politicians never admit to as a motive is the money. The favoured response at the moment is to say how they took a pay cut to come to Parliament. Alamein Kopu plays an interesting variation – she says she can't be doing it for the money because she's more broke on her parliamentary salary than she was on her benefit.

But the banal fact is that the money is quite good for many of them. And for some of them it's very good. Because it's called the public trough we assume it's full of food that pigs like. But – no, no, no – there is caviare and champagne in there for those who know how deep to plunge.

A third of all MPs used to be teachers, few of whom would have been making more than $45,000 a year. The basic parliamentary salary is $75,000 a year, but on top of that you get cheap food and wine, and a Wellington accommodation allowance. You get free taxis and free air travel for two anywhere in New Zealand (your spouse could, as some have been rumoured to do, run sales franchises all over New Zealand without paying for any travel)*. You'll bank more of your salary than in practically any job other than off-shore oil rigs.

MPs also get a parliamentary superannuation scheme which allows them to put aside some of their income (and some of ours as well). For every dollar they put in the taxpayer puts in another two. At the end of each three-year term parliamentarians can have an extra $50,000 tax-free in their fund.

Politicians are very far from indifferent to these inducements. The super scheme is particularly well thought of. It may even have contributed to Winston's decision to "seek a new mandate" by resigning from Parliament when the National Party expelled

* Every day some new perk comes to light. MPs get a thousand dollars a year in stamp warrants, originally for postage, now for anything sold in a post shop. That includes paying certain mortgages, buying bonus bonds, licensing your car, your television or paying your power bills.

him. As a resigning MP he was entitled to the benefits of the old super scheme that his colleagues had, and as a newly-elected MP he was also allowed to buy into the even more generous new pension scheme they had voted themselves in a two-minute motion one night.

Longer-serving parliamentarians have some awesome figures stacked up: Jonathan Hunt will have something around $600,000 in his fund which is available to him now if he retires, *along with* an annual state pension of over $62,000. Tirikatene Sullivan, Koro Wetere, Jim Bolger, Bill Birch, Mike Moore and someone called Warren Cooper are all around the half million mark with around $50,000 a year available to them as a pension.

If the lump sum is invested prudently, these people will have retirement incomes of around $100,000 a year. That is a serious incentive for many of us.

It's hard to believe that parliamentarians can be influenced by anything as banal as money. But the assumption that their minds are on higher things – the national debt, the surpluses, the trade-weighted index, the wine requirement in Bellamy's, the new accommodation for ministers, the optimal level of tax in the economy – is not always correct.

When the Nats were returned with a majority of one the time before last, Jim Bolger was serenely confident the government would run to full term. Why? "Because it's in no-one's interests to bring the government down," was his reasoning.

For me that didn't ring true. The Prime Minister was clearly wrong. It's always in the interests of the opposition to bring the government down, and as soon as possible, that's what the system is based on.

But underneath Bolger's subtle observation was the fact that sitting members would not endanger their superannuation by risking their seats in an election. If the government went to full term, each MP would benefit to the tune of $50,000 in their super fund. That was a powerful incentive to keep the boat afloat.

He tested his theory with a prediction. He reasoned the last thing the Labour Party wanted to do would be to sink the ship. Therefore he could approach the Labour Party for a Speaker – if they reduced their numbers (Speakers didn't vote in those days) it would give the government a working majority, and the Opposition could oppose without the fear of opposing so well that another election was necessary. None of Bolger's colleagues followed this argument – but he pulled it off when Peter Tapsell accepted the offer and gave the government its working majority.

3 The third thing you never hear politicians admit is, "I'm doing it for the status." Politicians may be despised and reviled in opinion polls, but when you meet a politician in real life, so to speak, few of us remain indifferent. You meet Maurice Williamson or even Simon Upton – and though they've done nothing of any moment for years, they are accorded respect. They are ministers of the crown. They see this respect in our eyes, and they like it.

It's also a great comfort when ignored at a party to be able to smile mysteriously and think, "How little these poor fools know! If they only suspected the half of it!"

From being a private professional – a teacher, an accountant, a trade union officer – you become elevated to being a public personage. You have opinions that might be quoted on national television. Things other people might say in saloon bars have a resonance when you utter them. If things go well, your wife can go shopping in a ministerial car (there is no greater luxury in city life than a chauffeur). You are literally part of the ruling class. You can snob your acquaintance, you travel first class for the first time in your life (unless you've been cabin crew). Parties are put on for you, at dinners you are on top table, the business elite are invited and you find that you are at least equal and sometimes above them in the seating plan. You are greeted when you arrive – and for a very gratifying reason. *It is because your worth has finally been recognised.*

And when you go out, people ask you what it's really like in Parliament and you can say: "Winston's a rogue all right, but a likeable one," or "Jim Bolger has a surprisingly substantial intellect, you know," or "Pam Corkery swears like a sewer worker but the microphones in the House don't pick it up," and nearly everyone will nod, grateful for insights into the secret society.

Has the status consciousness improved over the last thirty years? In the old days, Wellington was even more aware of the hierarchy than they are now. For instance, when the Labour government fell in '75, Zelda Finlay (cabinet minister Martyn Finlay's wife) was standing at a party in the James Cook. The wife of the then head of the Railways (the *Railways*!) looked her straight in the eye and said: "My husband and I are staunch National supporters," and she smiled thinly. "You mustn't expect that our association will continue now that your husband is no longer in government."

Finally, there is a more dangerously alluring temptation, most sinister in its action and its origins. MPs come to believe they are entrusted with the duty of articulating the hopes and fears of a generation, that they come to embody the whole essence of a constituency, a sort of minor version of a *L'etat, c'est moi* feeling. Symptoms of this madness can be observed when they start referring to themselves in the third person. You might call it Caesar's Disease. In his account of the Gallic wars Julius Caesar described his moving from one place to another by saying: *Caesar progressus est.* It is to stand somewhere other than where you are at the time and observe the majesty and destiny of yourself in action. Winston – in a whisky phase between two lite-beer phases – did it for a while: "Peters will never agree to that!" he'd say.

That is the start of the madness; when it ripens, that's when you will look in the mirror and see someone else looking back. And it's someone you like more than yourself!

But having said that, there is a reality underlying the illusions and delusions. As an MP you will be on the inside of the ring of fire at the centre of the national life. You will witness life-and-death struggles for power. You will see the classical, unchanging drama in the rise and fall of men and women aspiring to greatness. You will take sides. Even as a foot soldier you will help determine whether this country is wealthy or not (by voting taxes up or down). You will help determine whether we have a civil war or not (by how the Maori question is treated). These are great affairs of state you will personally witness.

And politicians see this reflected in the eyes of people they meet, for they are acutely sensitive to it. There are no greater things for New Zealanders to concern themselves with than these issues of national destiny. That's why there is no recovery. The attention, the influence, the power, the status has got into their bloodstream, into their bones, their soul, their genes, and there is no substitute, and usually no redemption.

2

What are they like?

SO, THE political are different. How different? Oh, they are very different. One interesting piece of evidence to clinch this is that normal people can't imitate them. New Zealand actors (not that you'd call actors normal, particularly) can do lunatics convincingly – but not politicians. Ian Mune's Muldoon, like Grant Tilly's or David McPhail's (or indeed, anyone's), was like Muldoon in the same way that minced meat is like roast beef. Even the least charismatic politician in Parliament is more authentically powerful than any local actor in a six-part series.

The English aren't that much better at it, truth to tell; it's not in the national character. Though it's worth recalling there have been a couple of breakthroughs recently: Ian Richardson in *House of Cards* had the psychopathic conviction, that inhuman coldness that qualified him. And Trevor Eve in *The Politician's Wife* also carried off the bluff vulgarity, the easy assumption that he was the most important person in the room.

And while they can do the structured authority of army officers, the English are much better at carrying off the feckless toffs of once-powerful families: Edward Fox as Edward VIII – that's far more part of the British national identity than the characters who successfully administer power. The English are graceful losers (so practised are they at it), not determined winners.

Not surprisingly, American film actors can do power characters much more naturally. This may be because they are better actors, but also the enormous fees they command mean they don't have to act so much. Their wealth and prestige put them in the bracket of nineteenth century dukes and duchesses – when you pay a large number of people to obey you in private life, you become used to command. So when they play senators, it shows.

When you have staff, when you go into shops people bob and curtsy, literally or metaphorically, it makes a difference to how you view yourself. This is what power does to you: it changes you so that you can easily believe you are the centre of everyone's world.

The British royal family have been in this peculiar position for two or three thousand years, so my genealogist tells me, and as a result are well decoupled from any reality we would regard as familiar. Twenty-five years ago, Prince Charles used to minimise the kiss-and-tell danger of a varied romantic life by preying on the wives of his friends; and he wouldn't do it in person but send an equerry to put the proposition ("Would you care to wait on HRH at so-and-so, at such-and-such a time?") *Apparently*, so I have been told by an old girlfriend, he used to like the female to cry out at his point of crisis: "*Thank* you sir! *Thank* you sir!"

If this is the sort of territory that power, prestige and position lead the hereditarily powerful – what chance do first generation, here-today-gone-tomorrow politicians have of keeping a grip on themselves?

Everyone's idea of a good politician would be someone clever, honest, hardworking with a varied background to provide them with experience of different conditions of life in New Zealand. Clem Simich, for instance, worked as a gumdigger in his youth, then became a stone-mason, and finally a policeman. He completed the fastest part-time law degree in New Zealand and worked tirelessly and faithfully for Rob Muldoon in Tamaki.

But he was sent to deliver a message to Wellington and was never heard of again.

The United Party was a group of decent, honest individuals from both sides of the political divide who genuinely felt they could create unity in the centre by co-operating with both sides. Any of them who stood in a contested seat sank without trace and I'd give ten dollars to anyone who could remember five of their names.

It takes a very specific person to go into politics, and do well once there. Say you had the intelligence, energy, and will; the experience, the charm, the persuasive abilities, the track record in the world to prove you know how business works; if you had these cherished endowments, why would you go into *politics*?

Let's look at Alan Gibbs. Here is a man of tigerish intelligence, explosive energy, and powerful will. His extraordinary wealth is only peripherally significant; that is, people don't listen to him just because he's rich.

On the face of it he would be better in Parliament than anyone. He can charm listeners into thinking his way, but he can also do the cold thing, or the angry thing. He changes colour, the eyes glare, an awesome stream of polemical argument issues. When he gets heated his veins pump up and attention heightens in his listeners.

Gibbs is the man who had Telecom staff levels halved after Troughton had already halved them saying further cuts were impossible. Gibbs bought Freightways without putting up any of his own money. Gibbs charmed a strike meeting of forestry workers in Reporoa and reversed their strike decision by saying to them: "There's only one question you've got to address tonight – do you want to be useless for the rest of your lives or do you want to do something useful?"

He's also had an incalculable influence backstage in the political theatre. When the Business Roundtable was being formed in the early '80s it was he who got the heavily-protected business community, the heavily licensed and subsidised establishment singing a free-market chorus. So when individual members of the group fell victim to market forces (and many did) the chorus kept singing, "market good, protection bad".

He has a primary political ability: he talks and people find themselves agreeing with him. There was a round table meeting of all Act's consultants, officers, politicians and researchers to straighten out the philosophical base of the party. He talked casually for twenty minutes and everyone agreed with him all the time; but he took the table from a communitarian position to free-market capitalism and back to communitarianism – very different philosophies – without any disagreement, or even any expressed recognition of the contradictions. He managed briefly to goad Roger Douglas into a limited response, but Roger has the economy of a great athlete – he runs only when there's a medal in it.

So why couldn't Gibbs be a parliamentary politician? There

are a number of reasons. He's probably too rude, even for a politician. That is, his wealth and intelligence have combined to make him eccentric by New Zealand norms. And also, there is a capriciousness in his nature which may be exacerbated by a lack of colleagues, or social controls (or friends, as they can also be known). This is a structural problem in New Zealand, by the way, and explains why talent frequently fails to achieve its potential. But first, foremost and finally – he doesn't want to. And why would he? Why would you? How could you want to trade your mornings and evenings driving to meetings to talk to people you've never met to submit your inner substance to the shopfront and have it fingered by sceptical and quality-conscious consumers?

Some people say we should pay more for parliamentarians because then we'd getter a better quality of politician. But would we, in fact? The occupation is a mystery, in the old guild sense. It is a secret society, joined by covert bonds and awful oaths of loyalty (if not to each other). However much they attack their opponents, however different their world view is, however ferociously they represent their constituents' interests – they have more in common with each other than they have with us.

That's worth unpacking: Jim Anderton has more in common with glamour-pants Peters than he does with the homeless, the downtrodden, the huddled masses of Sydenham. And while it's the last thing you expect, given all the hostility they display towards each other every day in Parliament, actually it's not surprising. They are creatures of their environment. They do things normal people wouldn't dream of.

Imagine: as a private citizen you're at home with your family wondering whether to have a second glass of wine before dinner. As an MP you are out in a snowstorm, driving two hours by yourself, to a hall you can't find in a place you've never heard of to address people you'll never meet again. You're running late because you're always late. Even if your speech is well received there'll be a grumpy old crank at the back who gets in a couple of heckles that find their mark, and it may be that old bat who misses her medication will somehow have found out where you're speaking. There'll be forty people there. Half of them will be party members (who don't count). If there is any media they will underestimate the audience number by half. The audience is polite but distant. When you look back on the evening, the admiration (if there was any) seems like a glass of water, and the two heckles that hit home are like fat blobs of ink discolouring the water. You spend the drive back constructing annihilating responses to the miserable old turkey who heckled you. And when you get back to base someone will say: "Well, we didn't like to say this, because you don't cope with criticism very well but . . . "

And someone else will chip in, "Was one of them a woman? You know you're not very good with women."

And someone else might say, "Why didn't you propose free childcare for working mothers, like I keep on suggesting?"

And you will find yourself thinking viciously the unforgivably vulgar thought, "Opinions are like arseholes. Everybody's got one," and wondering whether you dare say it.

You are now a public figure, you are up for constant inspection and appraisal. You have steeled yourself against intrusive coverage by the media (who, inexplicably, take no interest in you at all) but you hadn't counted on this chorus of critics in the office. As a senior politician you will have the protection of your praetorian guard but this far down in the system you are on your own. You are an owner-operator of your small political business surrounded by competitors and colleagues who would not grieve if you came to grief. Even your closest political colleagues realise that if you are higher on the party list they will be lower. There is a motto that you come to fear is true: "There is no more subtle pleasure in life than seeing your best friend fall off a roof."

It is this realisation that encourages you to have another drink. Drinking is an ever-present condition in politics, and this is one advantage to the industry. It is a job, like journalism, that you can do while wholly intoxicated. There are those who say that heavy drinking never solves anything but we know that's simply not true.

No wonder politicians have more in common with each other than they have with us. None of us go through these painful, humiliating and frankly exhausting experiences day after day, as a matter of routine.

It may be worth casting upwards from these grass-roots beginnings to note that leaders are stranger even than the rank and file. When Derek Quigley was standing up to Muldoon the story has it that he had lunch with Bob Jones to discuss his leadership potential. "You'll never lead the National Party," Bob said.

"But why do you say that?" Derek is said to have replied, with some indignation.

"Take your glasses off and I'll tell you," Bob said, and when Derek took the glasses off, Bob went on, "If I'd told Muldoon to take his glasses off like that he'd have told me to get bent. That's why he's the leader of the National Party and you'll never be."

Leaders *are* like that, actually. If you'd told Prebble to take his glasses off he'd just look at you. Bolger would say, "Now, why would I want to take my glasses off, I wonder?" And Lange would have said, "If you think taking my glasses off will help you see straight you're nuttier than you look, Bob."

Leaders are the centre of the mystery; they carry the party balance in their heads; they weigh the information only they have; they can never give themselves to any of the factions; they have an impregnability; they are without weakness, there are no breaches in their dykes, they are a mystery all of their own.

That's why, when we unpack it further, different levels of two political hierarchies are closer to each other than they are to their respective junior colleagues. Therefore leader Jim Anderton is not only closer to leader Winston than to his voters, he is also closer to Winston than he is to his finance spokesperson.

It's impossible to test this theory thoroughly because the only people who have the inside knowledge wouldn't know if it were true or not. But it is observably true that leaders have this added remoteness over and above the normal remoteness that politicians have already.

They also do things even politicians don't have to do. They have to look after their caucuses with all their frictions and factions. The tensions are frequently serious. When Prebble came in to lead Act, I started to tell him how dysfunctional the place was, how no-one passed through the party with their reputations better than when they went in, how none of us in any of the factions had ever worked in such an organisation, how hard it was to get *typing* done, he airily dismissed it: "Oh, it's always like this in political parties," he said. Mind you, he'd come out of the Labour Party where an internecine battle between Old Labour, New Labour and the Rogernomic Rump was the daily fare.

Be that as it may, political leaders are different from

administrative leaders, and leaders in power may be very different from leaders in opposition.

Isolation adds more perils to leaders' lives. But one thing leaders have is a weakness for the loyalists they gather around them.

In larger parties, loyalty is more important than intelligence. This was observed in Muldoon's day by the appointment of a succession of duds to important positions. Their ability to run a ministry was less important than their willingness to support the leader. In a perverse way, it can still be true that the very *lack* of ability is an important part of their political qualifications. Able people feel less obligation for the position – they assume they deserve their promotion. Incapable place-holders know they are there only by the grace and favour of their benefactor.

These incapable loyalists constitute a praetorian guard who can be relied on to ward off challenges; they can constitute a flying squad, or a tight five. They speak up in cabinet, caucus and in meetings. If you want to criticise the leader, the leader won't have to reply to you personally. The guards pile into you first. They can be rewarded – at a local level chairmen of electorate committee can have the seat bestowed on them by a grateful retiring member (Brian Talboys did for Derek Angus, David Thompson did for Roger Maxwell and Sir Robert Muldoon did for Clem Simich – it doesn't seem to be a particularly good idea when we look at it).

But in their way, they isolate the leader as much as anything else. It's an occupational hazard. Prime ministers are always in danger of becoming remote from their ministers. The impression of Jim Bolger's relationship with his cabinet was of a medieval king operating in a baronial system. A distant and uneasy relationship (barons gang up sometimes and put in one of their own kind).

It was something similar in earlier days. While Muldoon had a praetorian guard of loyalists and other incompetents (remember the minister of transport who was legendarily stupid) he became increasingly remote. It became both a symptom and a cause of the final stages of his megalomania.

He was supplanted by David Lange's government; anyone of conscious age must remember the relief of Lange after the bitterness of the Muldoon years. Lange was young, refreshing, and widely thought of as a great wit (Certainly! *Wombat!*" he said to an Australian journalist who'd asked for a word). He was communicative where Muldoon had been laconic and open where Muldoon had been paranoid. What a relief it was. And yet within three or four years Lange was as remote as any leader had ever been. He was found once by the fire brigade, unconscious on his bed, alone and in his underpants, with a burning mess of baked beans on the stove. It was a picture of desolation quite equal to the image of Muldoon, rotten with gin, slumped alone on the floor by his office fridge, being helped to a seat by his President of the National party, Sue Wood.

In Roger Douglas' paper delivered to cabinet he shows the reality of the leader's isolation, and how Lange quite against the odds had come to take on the autocratic mantle of the previous prime minister: "Does the prime minister not believe in the cabinet process? Does he automatically take it for granted that he has a monopoly of wisdom in cases of disagreement? Has he some difficulty in allowing other people to review the quality of his case? Can he not bear the idea of losing?"

Jim Bolger, while remote from his colleagues, has been famously loyal to them. Even when Simon Upton, desperate to get out of the Bermuda Triangle which constitutes the health portfolio, tried to resign over the 'bad blood' scandal in which a number of people died, Bolger would not let him go. Once you're in, you're in; you're part of the leader's mindset; if you have to go you're better to wither in situ than remove yourself and disturb the intricate placement he's gone to such pains to arrange.

Some people (and not just politicians) say we should pay them $250,000 a year. Certainly, pay for MPs is relatively declining. In 1972 they were paid almost three times the national average, now it's just over double.

Commonsense as much as economic theory (both frequently unreliable guides), suggests that the pay must have a bearing on the calibre of people the industry attracts. It's said in America that the top executives don't run for President because winning would interfere with their careers. But then there is a serious point: would the people attracted by the higher salaries be any good at politics?

This is an occupation, remember, where Mike Moore is a better player than Doug Myers. This is a game where Richard Prebble beats Alan Gibbs. This is an arena where Trevor Mallard does better than . . . well, let's not over-egg the pudding. It's enough to say that success in other fields does not equip you for success in politics.

This is not to say everyone in Parliament is of this high calibre, but not everyone in Parliament is a politician. In the same way there are very few scientists. The numbers in the populous scientific establishment are made up of technicians who busy themselves tabulating results to support or attack that which scientists have discovered. In the same way, there are very few politicians – people who have a vision, who create, who impress their ideas on the minds of those around them.

Similarly, most of the populous political establishment

consists of managers and administrators, the professional advocates, the on-the-one-hand consultants, the shadow boxers, the seat warmers. Some of these people can, as pointed out earlier, be senior apparatchiks in the administration. They have the political equivalent of the pointless good looks that some actors suffer from (the missing ingredient for actors is sex appeal). When you are attacked by a real politician it hurts – and the reason is, they can persuade you that their punch carries behind it the power and force of public opinion. They can hit you with a whole constituency.

There was at least one interesting observation in *The Spin*: the inventory of a politician's personality is very similar to that of a psychopath's. Both sorts see the world only in terms of themselves; they never admit they are wrong; they never apologise; they never express gratitude; a sense of conflict is central to their view of the world. They live in a different reality from the rest of us.

What it is – politicians are inclined to believe they are featuring in a film; it is the film of their lives. In fact, they are starring in this film. As they go about their daily business, the soundtrack is thundering in their ears, and everywhere they turn there are bit players supporting the action; the only purpose of these mechanicals is to assist the denouement – which is always the triumph of the star. In this state of being the world is what you think it is. It is a world you can create by thinking it. In legal language this usually translates as 'guilty but insane'.

There is a further similarity between these two sets of humans. From personal experience I know something about paranoids – having lived and worked with them. I find paranoid women, particularly, so attractive that I can't afford to have anything to do with them any more. I'm like an alcoholic who can't even have a beer. For a period before this rule, I lived with a minor psycho. She was glamorous, exciting, extraordinarily beautiful – but afflicted. She caused fights at parties and so forth; she spoke to people as if she was watching them on television: "*God* you're ugly!" she said meeting a rough-hewn friend of mine for the first time. But no matter how she insulted and abused people she was always shocked when they snapped back. Because she was unable ever to take the blame for anything she had constantly to reconstruct the past to cast herself in the role of injured party. This became more than fancy footwork – the constant reconstruction of reality created a fantasy life that only looked like the world where the rest of us lived. This paranoid creation is the same world that politicians live in. Indeed, she it was who taught me what has become the First Law of Darkness (q.v.)

In describing what politicians need to be like to it may be worth saying what they're not like. As vampires don't have shadows, some of the absences in the political inventory are giveaways.

Hate would, you'd think, be an occupational necessity for the business they're in. They're immersed in conflict, their business days are filled with strike and counter-strike. And as they live in close inspection of the damage their opponents are doing to society – how couldn't they hate?

When you look at how Helen Clark and Jim Anderton have denounced the government on behalf of the poor and the voiceless – how can they not be feeling this fundamental emotion? They look over their depressed constituencies and see the decline in their quality of life, the houses of gathering squalor, abuse, joblessness, hopelessness – how can they not hate the perpetrators? When you remember what Winston has said, and his manner of saying it – the frauds, the conspiracies, the deception, the lies, the "evil" National government – but then quite abruptly he and his enemy are new best friends, sitting up till late talking intimately about their fathers.

Two things: i) it's the flick on the nose that enrages people more than the big body blows. It was only when Mike Moore called Jim Bolger "thick" that Bolger threw his pen across the floor of the House ("*Wooo* bait!"). The trivial often has a greater effect on political careers than the substantial (see the Third Law of Darkness).

And ii) what looks like hate is actually anger. Winston the outsider railed against the National hierarchy because he felt despised by it. The word was that he had heard a senior member of the hierarchy say, "Get the little Maori boy to do it."

But now, as Treasurer, Birch's boss and Deputy Prime Minister he has the respect of his colleagues; he has beaten them all. He left in disgrace, he went into the wilderness, he returned in triumph. The immediate source of his anger is healed. And indeed he now projects a rather unearthly calm, as though he's having an out-of-body experience. When I've spoken to him recently, he talks as if his ambitions have been fulfilled (well, half of them must have been, at least). He said, "You must remember, Simon, that I've been at four per cent twice before."

He is fully confident he will rise again, and I have to say it wouldn't be surprising if he did. There are significant economic bonuses coming down the track over the next three years – there are all those international sports events and millennial celebrations, and more significantly, New Zealand may be allowed to join the American trading bloc. The economic boost from these events will be working in favour of the current leadership; this is worth remembering.

So what do you need to be a politician? There are a number of qualities and skills of different kinds you'll either have or acquire. The trouble is that all the qualities you need for the peculiar occupation you've chosen are qualities that divorce you from your psychological origins.

Tough:

Does your stomach get fluttery when conflict approaches? Does the phrase "I've got a bone to pick with you" make you anxious? Do you know what you actually think about things? Have you examined all the angles of what you know to defend yourself from an unexpected quarter?

You have to be tough. Alamein Kopu was right (no seriously). So was Rana Waitai. It's a den of lions in Parliament; you need warrior virtues to prosper there, you need to be indomitable. It's this toughness that allows politicians to create the world in their own image, to create a vision large enough for their supporters to live in, and to defend it against all attacks.

Thus, Paul Holmes takes possession of the most damaging report on Winston's Winebox – it effectively demolishes his credibility and he asks Winston on air whether he's going to apologise to one of the civil servants whose career he has ruined. Winston's opening response will be a useful model for you to follow. He said: "What did the Commissioner just say? I'll tell you what he just said. We just heard him say that paying tax is voluntary! I'm not going to agree with that, and neither are millions of ordinary New Zealanders." That's tough.

He coined another beauty when he said, "People who call the ATN scandal a matter of morality and ethics simply underscore how tacky, tasteless and shallow they have allowed themselves to become." That's really tough.

You have to like winning arguments; you have to enjoy

bending people to your will and not feeling obligated to them. You have to have character enough to carry strangers to your position and not feel you've done them a violence; lesser people may persuade someone to their point of view, but then feel they have to let them win something back (see Fourth Law – at the point of victory you are at your weakest).

You have to aspire to the condition of those barristers who actually enjoy bullying witnesses to a conclusion: "You can't deny X? Then you must agree with Y! Therefore you will have to confess to Z! *Confess damn you, you've already admitted it!*"

To launch a sustained assault on your opposite number as Helen Clark did in the shadow health portfolio you need the warrior capacity sitting schizo alongside the ability to be at peace and in good humour.

You need the confidence, the resilience, the hide, the capacity to take criticism without caring. This is not normal. Most of us look for approval. Most of us feel upset when a motorist blows his horn at us.

New Zealand, at an earlier stage of individuation than Britain, has for years been a country over-eager for approval. In London the driving is very co-operative but the conversation is very competitive; in New Zealand the driving is homicidally competitive but conversation is depressingly co-operative ("That's right, that's right," people say when I run this line, "You're right, we don't contradict each other enough.") While New Zealanders are the most winnowing gossips in the world (you can find out everything you need to know about a stranger in half a dozen phone calls) they are equally reluctant to express a contrary view in front of their conversation partners. New Zealanders view conversation as a venture into uncertain territory where it's important to keep together. (Even Richard Prebble rarely contradicts you outright. "Let me put another thought to you," he says, when you're talking nonsense.)

So New Zealand doesn't have that obnoxious, ruling-class tradition in its private education system where boys and girls are trained to stand up and stand out with their opinions. As this is the first demand of public life, politicians are even more peculiar in this country than they are elsewhere. So it takes a particular courage, or recklessness or, at worst, insensitivity to proceed as a politician. When the habit gets engrained it can start reducing the quality of private life.

Standing out from the crowd has never been a characteristic of this country, because though the media clobbering machine is quite benign, the clobbering at a personal level is very thorough.

David Kirk has said he overheard a group of rugby supporters talking about him. "Isn't that David Kirk? What's he, Labour or National?"

"National, he was."

"Yes, bright c#@!, wasn't he?"

There is a deep need for New Zealanders to stick together in the forwards, as it were, to keep together because there really is safety in numbers. Even in Parliament the pressure works more than you might assume. Jim Anderton was recently lobbying support for his bill to give dead soldiers medals and John Banks said he'd vote for it if Act voted for it, but not if they didn't. Why would bite-the-bullet Banks care which way Act was voting, you'd wonder?

And of course it's not unique to New Zealand. Clive James, the Australian television critic and performer, was asked twenty years ago to sign a petition to get a prisoner pardoned. His first question wasn't to enquire about the man or what he had or hadn't done. His first question was: "Who else has signed it?" And on being told, he came back a few days later with the decision: "My agent has advised me it wouldn't be a good idea to be associated with these people at this stage in my career."

Given this pacific tendency, it took a special quality, largely unrecognised, for Jim Bolger to take on responsibility for his first-term government's extraordinary unpopularity, and to withstand the maelstrom of media vengeance that erupted around them all.

Bolger appeared on the *Holmes* show at a time when the media feeling was at its height – employment contracts had just come in, benefits had been cut, we lost an important rugby test to Australia and the murder rate had leapt up. In fact, we'd had a full year's murders in the first four months. "What do you want me to do about it?" Bolger eventually asked after an excoriating line of questions. "*Give them some jobs!*" Holmes yelped. And there was no answer for so silly an exclamation. They're the best of friends now, of course, the last I heard.

But there are few people in private life who wouldn't be damaged by this, to be denounced on national television as the person responsible for a massive increase in the murder rate. It's something that would keep us awake at night. It's like being mugged. But then, boxers find it less distressing getting into a street fight because they're used to violence. For us peaceful types, were we mugged we wouldn't go outside for a month.

Winston has this quality in great measure; he has been in the wilderness, shunned by his colleagues, trying to put the machinery of a political party together (something he has no talent for), and not only survived but succeeded.

Prebble must have the same degree of hide to have turned twenty-two state organisations from woeful losers into respectable trading organisations, and to have managed the redundancy of tens of thousands of state employees.

Jim Anderton must have enormous reserves of stamina and

guts to keep the nitwits of his far-flung alliance in line with the less absurd. Alamein complains he called her "ignorant". ("Good grief," he must have thought, "that was being *nice* to her!")

Mike Moore must have substantial resources to keep his courage when all around were whispering and the white ants were whittling invisibly away at his leadership.

Lange took it for a while, then quit.

Enduring politicians have to develop the protective calluses; in extreme cases they grow an exo-skeleton, like crabs. But down in the other end of the pool where the beginners splash about, it is that much more obvious how gruelling the occupation of politics is.

Denis Welch says that the intensity of party politics is in inverse proportion to the amount of power the party has achieved. The Alliance internal politics were intense, more so than anything previously experienced – but the Alliance had an MP, a leader, an established power base, and twenty per cent of the vote.

On that scale, imagine how intense were the internal politics of Act with only an interim leader, no MPs and polling one per cent. From my experience it can be said that no organisation has had such a vivid emotional life. It required resilience all round, more than any other experience (and I speak for all of us) to avoid total nervous collapse.

Act had made the mistake of assuming people would be interested in the launch and progress of a new political party. In the event, the lack of attention was overwhelming.

Roger Douglas' rally in Otara (which attracted a thousand people) was reported only insofar as there were scuffles. The party's unpaid presence in the media was negligible. And it does take a toughness to deal with the daily failure to be noticed; to be so insignificant that your opponents don't attack you. One faction in the party dealt with the problem by affecting a sort of pained silence, refraining after a while even from putting out press statements about the power of compound interest.

It is important to have a boxfile of policy documents, especially one that emits a mysterious light to draw pilgrims in their hundreds from all over the country. Policy certainly adds an interesting dimension to party politics. But pilgrims are eccentric by their nature, and unreliable voters. And the political process being what it is, the fine print of the policy is never going to be implemented. The reality is that parties need some additional way of communicating with the public.

Call me old-fashioned but regularly appearing in the paper or on the news helps show voters what you are about. It may be that no-one takes any notice beyond the fact that you are featured, but if you can be seen holding the severed arm of your enemy, or a readily-recognisable equivalent, you will be delivering a message of some sort, and that is significant.

It is necessary that people know of you to vote for you; they need to see you in action and test your mettle. While this wasn't the popular argument in the party at the time it wasn't an argument that had to be won; the way things worked, if you wanted to do something there wasn't anyone who could give you permission to do it. You just did it.

News releases, I came to see, had a better chance of being printed if they contained news. We should therefore identify news stories and package new information in a newsworthy way. So, the early search was for an issue to dramatise the party position – and first up was government waste. The dispute around Tamaki Girls College with its protesters and disproportionate security presence offered the stage on which we might attempt a suitable drama.

You may remember that the ten-acre site was threatened by Maori protesters, and the Ministry of Education sent in the police with a back-up of dozens of private security guards at an extraordinary expense (there were up to thirty guards holed up in the school buildings: the vigil outside the perimeter fence consisted of two protesters and their dog. The security people occasionally used to feed them).

After considerable research, official information probes, investigation in and around the security industry (which has its own atmosphere of paranoia to cope with), Rodney Hide got the costs of the security up in the media, along with a variety of colourful and media-friendly questions about whether the guards were licensed, whether a female guard had been molested, whether one of them had been caught one night on the playing fields performing an act too indecent to mention here, and whether there was a plot to bus in more protesters to justify the security presence. All these questions had been uncovered by enquiries on the telephone and down there face to face on-site.

The coverage generated wasn't enormous, but it was Act's first appearance in the media participating in a current event. We had two or three full pages in *Truth* and some reluctant coverage in the *Herald*. We had an interaction with the apparatus of state from an unfamiliar angle, one that would be familiar to criminals or spies, perhaps.

But the first lesson of politics is a harsh one, and what it does is require you not to look for applause from your colleagues; even looking for approval sets you up for punishment. The Tamaki coverage produced the following views: "Are we sure this is the right thing to be doing? Isn't it getting people's backs up? Won't it confuse people if we attack National? Our supporters don't read *Truth*, do they? Aren't people sick of aggressive politics? You're getting up some very serious people's noses, you know? Isn't it better to run the story in a hot medium like radio? It's not helping us in the polls at all, is it? Can't we be above all this? Should we be appearing in the paper at all? Are you running all your press releases through a lawyer? Remember what happened last time? Mate, are you sure you're taking the strain all right? Shouldn't you have a holiday?"

Criticism from every quarter constitutes real pressure when you aren't used to it; and probably when you are used to it, it doesn't get markedly easier because the pressure is more skilfully applied. Neil Kirton would be feeling it, it takes fortitude to withstand it; Winston and Jim Anderton from their respective positions would know all about it, Michael Laws knows it, Jim Bolger knew it through his first two years as Prime Minister, clearly Roger Douglas and Richard Prebble would have – even Alamein Kopu has felt it. You carry on every day, walking through a fog of widely-felt hostility, and you carry yourself as though you were well-liked and respected.

Parliament is the wrestling cage where weakness and toughness contend. What is being searched out? Not answers to the big questions, but chinks in the armour, in order to get a wedge in and try and make a split obvious. The barrage of heckling is to try and discover a weak point, any weak point – it might only be discernible as a flaring of the nostrils. But if you haven't got the ability to bruise interjectors, to damage those hecklers and comedians they will take liberties with you.

Muriel Newman asked a question: "Does the minister have an opinion on the figure of $10,000 a minute to run Parliament or a million dollars a minute?" Winston stood up instead and asked, "Does the minister have an opinion on the boatshed in Whangarei that's been illegally built?" (Muriel had had a little local difficulty along those lines.) Her question was lost.

When she asked a question about costs for a social welfare conference, Roger Sowry said, "Is this the member who told an old woman to pose naked for extra cash?" (a reference to a media interpretation from one of Muriel's *Oily Rag* books). Her question again was lost.

These head-high tackles are the daily routine of parliamentary life, and it does take a coarsening of the spirit to withstand.

There was a Japanese POW commandant who was most feared because he was able to find out the particular fear of each man. And that's what Parliament does (you thought it was to process legislation?) It is the Room 101 where you confront your fears. And it might be something as basic as "Winston! You're short!" Or "Tuku! Your dad's from Rarotonga!" Or "Banks! What's the weather like in Queensland!" Here more than anywhere you need the carapace to protect yourself and your party. To be abashed in Parliament is obvious. When Deb Morris or Neil Kirton do badly in the House, the National backbench enjoy it in one way, but in a larger sense are diminished.

Most of us haven't felt the power of public opinion as directly as this since we were at school, in the playground. Before we smile, therefore, at Sharon Crosbie's observation about the roomful of toddlers, we should cast back and remember how well we dealt with it ourselves, in the playground, during our brief periods when everybody hated us.

On a personal note, the reason why I would never go into politics is the lack of this primary quality. When I used to play chess at school winning was harder than losing. Lacking a killer instinct I had to force myself to chant "inevitable consequences", in order to play my best move. It was awful to be engaged in a close game with your seniors when they weren't up to it (you have to know how humiliating it is to lose at chess). Twenty years ago playing against Bob Jones in Wellington it was clear he wasn't quite as good as I was, but he beat me three times in a row: it just took too much toughness to watch Bob lose.

Individuals need to be tough, and so do parties. They need to retain their integrity (an odd word, you might think to use in this context, but it is used in a special sense). Parties must keep their wholeness; like cells have a cell wall which defines their boundaries. Everything outside the cell wall is other and essentially hostile. Therefore, going into coalition with a larger party and being absorbed by their collective responsibility is very dangerous, even for a party with as much definition as New Zealand First (for United it was fatal).

The rule that can be drawn from this is that smaller parties should remain outside the government and decide whether to support them issue by issue. A flighty mistress usually gets more attention than a faithful wife.

It's interesting to speculate why more National MPs don't do a Neil Kirton or a Michael Laws. Why doesn't Clem or Brian or Wayne say they are going back to their electorate to consult them on the importance of reviving the tax cuts? Why wouldn't they focus attention on themselves for a year, making their support for the government conditional on their terms?

I fear the answer is only too obvious.

Frightening:

The ability to frighten people is an interesting fundamental of the dark art. We can divide politicians into those who can frighten people and those who can't.

Richard Prebble, Alan Gibbs, Rob Muldoon – they're

frightening. Bob Jones probably used to be able to do it a bit. Winston also on his day can land punches that leave even stalwart bruisers breathless. He certainly seemed to connect with John Banks that brawling night when he said: "If you don't shut up I'll say what I know about *Queensland Banksie*." We never did find out what that was about. We never even found out whether the punctuation made a difference. "I'll say what I know about Queensland, Banksie," implies a one-off incident, whereas Queensland Banskie suggests such repetitive behaviour that it's become a nickname.

Jim Bolger's not frightening, David Lange wasn't frightening. Why are some people frightening? You feel some raw primal substance coming off them. Muldoon was frightening. Even the idea of him is frightening. That old quip, "There's no arguing with him. If his pistol misfires he knocks you down with the butt end of it," is correct. He was the embodiment of fear: his disproportionately large head, mottled with darkness, was like something out of *Jurassic Park II.* Bob Jones seems able to admire him perhaps because he wasn't frightened of him. It's as well the population was more timorous than Bob otherwise Muldoon would have had to rouse himself to greater feats of fear-mongering (imagine the darkness of his last decade combined with the power of the decade before).

Back to reality: I always thought Doug Graham might have the potential for inspiring fear (there's something Scorpio about his eyes) but nothing he's done so far suggests he has.

Donna Awatere Huata has it but doesn't use it.

What is it? Even a sense of purpose is unsettling these days, a sense that the purpose is equipped with experience, drive and confidence to move the argument, that's impressive. This sense of engagement underneath the argument is powerful. Very few politicians hit a ruck expecting to move it. Only the very effective ones land blows that actually hurt.

Incidentally, people who were there say that you could never be entirely confident that Robert Maxwell wouldn't hit you during a business negotiation (that adds a wholly new dimension to a meeting). This may be why Muldoon punched that photographer on the tarmac by the plane that time. He got a reputation with very little physical risk (when it comes to throwing punches the element of surprise is always on the side of the Minister of Finance).

But Muldoon's effect was on a different level than anything you find today. He had a unique malevolence but it was matched with an actual capacity to damage – that's what made him frightening. All power is a bluff, it is said. But that's one of those statements that is true but useless.

People are frightened of a number of things: surveys tell us that the fear-factor of speaking in public is rated higher than death. So being successfully mocked, being laughed at by a scornful audience is something most people will do anything to avoid. Muldoon was particularly accomplished in the arts of mockery. Ironically, his two most celebrated *bon mots* came from a very specific source. The first described Bill Rowling as "a set of shivers looking for a spine to crawl up"; the second occurred when wishing an Australian *bon voyage* from New Zealand to Australia and he was able to say: "Now the IQ of both countries will rise." Both these shafts, interestingly in the light of what later developed between them, were a couple of hoary Oxford Union jokes given to Muldoon in a private audience with Simon Walker.

Muldoon was said to have had a great sense of humour, but probably this was over-rated. When the great and good attempt even modest jokes, their audience is so grateful they tend to overestimate the actual comedy content. He had a sense of scorn which when administered in the approved way had the appearance of humour in those knockabout days.

There was an incident when a Labour member, Frank Rogers, had been in an altercation with a taxi driver. Shortly after this, Frank heckled Muldoon in Parliament; the old tusker paused, the chamber hushed in anticipation; he said: "Heh heh – *Taxi Frank*." This is the legendary counterpunch (am I alone in thinking it's not very good?) In Hastings he was heckled from the back of the stalls. He says, "There's one of those university students." The audience roars with laughter. You probably had to be there.

The other powerfully humiliating experience is being crushed in an argument on intellectual grounds (it's like losing at chess, one of the most personal and aggressive forms of single combat). Muldoon had the intellect to construct an argument with crushing power and the emotional apparatus to deploy it.

But as his megalomania developed he also developed a more sophisticated capacity for threatening his enemies in a vague and sinister way. When a council committee passed a hostile resolution he said: "I know who these people are, I've called for a list of their names." This is the line favoured by anonymous telephone maniacs: they croak into the phone, "I know where you live," and you worry for the safety of your wife and children. When you are stalked by a tiger in the jungle, you can never tell exactly where the growls are coming from – they seem to surround you. So it was with Muldoon and his Mob. The impression of being outnumbered was more real than apparent: his followers and appointees even started to *talk* like him (Morrie Davis at Air New Zealand being a prime example). In a real sense he was everywhere.

It's impossible to explain the effect of Muldoon to young people today. They think of it in terms of, "Jim Bolger calls for a list of our names? Like, we care?" You tell them that his grip on the establishment was so strong that Peter Cook's song *Spotty Muldoon* was banned in the run-up to an election – then the young ones really look at you sideways and wonder if you're all there.

Muldoon's techniques were of his time when employers were few and most professional opportunities were in their gift. The economy was heavily regulated – a system of monopolies was granted to businessmen which allowed them to be the sole importer or manufacturer, or service agent in their field.

If you offended Muldoon your colleagues and professional contacts would know that to favour you (with a job, a licence, a commission) would be to taunt the Prime Minister. So he had a personal capacity to damage your career, your well-being.

He was a man brimming with personal power. Here was a man who, when asked a question on television, would turn to the camera with the red light on and address his reply straight to the viewers. The producers sat in their glass cage and watched their interviewers reduced to a functionary, but they never had the courage to switch cameras while he was talking. This would have provided the nation with the satirical picture of a man talking in profile into the void. But then, such a producer would have found himself relegated within six months to afternoon women's programmes as a prelude to being bounced out of the service altogether.

The paranoia in television at the time was intense. Ian Cross used to argue persuasively against the TV terrorist genre championed later by Bill Ralston. And he'd argue not that it was bad television, or even undesirable, but he'd use the dark argument that it didn't help him in his struggle to keep the integrity of publicly-funded television. It was a collaborator's argument, and there is a Vichy sense that still colours talk of that time. No-one admits to being frightened by the old brute, no-one admits to collaborating. But until Simon Walker conducted the famous interview about the presence or absence of Russian warships in the Indian Ocean, no-one had ever contradicted the Prime Minister on television (indeed, one of the other gun interviewers of the time was required not just to ask the questions but also to prepare the coffee for the interviewee).

In the first current affairs interview shown on British television the interviewer (in evening dress) asked Sir Anthony Eden the following incisive question: "Prime Minister, you are well known for your expertise in foreign affairs but your knowledge of domestic matters is also very impressive. Which would you like to talk about first?" That ethos still had echoes in New Zealand twenty years later.

Walker was twenty-three and looked younger; Muldoon was at the height of his vigour. Walker questioned whether the named Russian ship actually existed – the editor of *Jane's Fighting Ships* said it did not. An astonished Muldoon declared Walker to be "a nitpicker" and prepared to read out and answer the next question on the list that had been prepared for him. Walker dug his heels in with the remark that became famous, "With respect, Prime Minister . . . " He said, "With respect Prime Minister, this is my interview and I shall ask the questions in the order I see fit. Now the Russian ship that you say was . . . "

The interview made the front page for a week, and for three weeks after that the letters columns of the *Listener* and the dailies were full of it. We forget the catharsis of the time – someone had persistently contradicted the Prime Minister on television and got away with it. For many people it was like seeing their father in a fight in the pub.

For that was how it was in New Zealand in those days. No-one had the weight to nail Muldoon in argument until David

Lange. Muldoon was free to say whatever it occurred to him to say. He once quipped that if America had used the ultimate weapon in Vietnam they wouldn't have lost the war there. Geoff Gerard had earlier said in Singapore that you had to drop "a basketful of bombs on Asians because that's all they understand," and he'd been packed off to Canada as high commissioner as punishment. Muldoon's remark was rather more serious, it was thought, but he easily dismissed the ensuing protests by repeating words to the effect of, "I never said nuclear weapon! I said ultimate weapon! Not the same thing at all!" It was the equivalent at the time of Winston's "Read the speech! I never said what you think I said!"

In Britain, Muldoon went through an experience of Gulliver in the land of the giants when David Dimbleby, doyen of liberal interviewers, asked him about his nuclear advice. After the PM blustered, Dimbleby said with a marvellously weary nonchalance, "Prime Minister, I think we both know what you mean when you say the words 'ultimate weapon'".

Bob Jones is leading his revisionist movement for Muldoon but he was a man who had looked into the abyss. Every man gets the face he deserves, it is said, and his face was brutally descriptive of his character; he had a face like the portrait of Dorian Gray. All his weaknesses and vices were there for all to see – for strong liquor, cruelty, power, paranoia. He was monstrously impressive.

After Simon Walker, and of course Derek Quigley, there was one person who really did stand up to Muldoon, and that was Ruth Richardson. Ruth took him on, in the public privacy of caucus, and did so nose to nose.

John Banks tells a story about the first caucus meeting. Ruth has come to see him the night before. Banks is the bouncy young right-winger who wants tax rates at twenty per cent and a winding-back of the state. Ruth is lining him up to support her attack on Muldoon: "There are two sorts of politicians," she tells him, and you can hear her saying it, "those with spines of steel and those with spines of jelly." (It's one of the unfair prerogatives of the writer that we can pass olympian judgments on Ruth as "naive"; frontal assaults are naive (see Laws Six and Seventeen) and it is immensely to her credit how well she eventually did.)

So Ruth launched her attack in front of all her colleagues and sat down. Muldoon looked around the caucus room with his frightening blue eyes, cold and angry, and settled on our hero: "You want to contribute to this debate, Banks?" he asked, and Banks suddenly found that he did not.

This story is told in Paul Goldsmith's book (Banks' press secretary during the time of writing), and the important point, removing Paul's capable spin, is that Banks – the black-and-white man, the bullet-biter, the battler – funked it. The old boar had merely to point his tusks towards the young man to dominate him.

Frightening, you see, which is how Muldoon started us down a path that many Latin American countries went down, and he did it, essentially by using this most impressive ability.

Showing your temper is a useful ability in politics. People don't like being shouted at. Drill sergeants in the army used to stand very close to shout at you because they knew you can reorganise someone's mind if you can hit them directly in the brain – your voice goes *in* through the eyes and becomes part of your cortex.

It is important to remember that losing your temper and shouting is always a transforming experience for those around you. Either you will succeed in instilling fear, and they will be reluctant to contradict you again, *or* you will become a figure of ridicule, because as every married man knows, he never looks so ridiculous as when he throws a tantrum. A tantrum can be defined as a loss of temper beyond your ability to lose temper – punching above your emotional weight.

But why is temper, properly exposed, so impressive? The plasma that is released is a substance that civilised people spend their formative years learning to conceal. To expose this substance introduces a random element into the room, and people become wary when they don't know what is going to happen next.

There are a number of other qualities politicians find useful.

• *Voice.* You need a vocal technique that converts as much breath to voice as possible. A good half of your personal image will come from your voice – a fact that is observable in plain but successful newsreaders. Roger Douglas can talk at an ordinary conversational level and be heard at the back of an audience of two hundred. Muldoon had a voice that could corkscrew its way through the roar of Parliament. Winston's voice, like a bucket of gravel shaken in the public's face, is as serious as it's thrilling.

• *Paranoid instincts.* Good politicians are always wary of being ambushed.

Lew Grade was asked "what's two and two?" He said, "Buying or selling?"

The political equivalent is the question: "Can you trust them?"

The answer is: "To do what?"

You're a politician. Your friends and colleagues say they're on your side, and they may be; they probably are (they're your friends and colleagues after all). But how much are they on your side? Will they speak out for you? And if so, where? At the bar? In an office? In the boardroom? And will they speak out for you in a way that commits their prestige to your position? Will they die in a ditch for you? Or will they suddenly succumb to your opponents' argument ("I must say, that *is* a point worth looking at") and scupper your entire plan? (See Second Law, friends more dangerous than enemies).

We can't know how reliable our colleagues are until we've been through the fire – and then we only know that we've gone through a fire together, not whether we'll go through another.

Also having a feel for paranoia allows you to administer it effectively. The correct administration of paranoia is among the most important political abilities.

We can all take criticism in varying degrees from our friends and family, but funnily enough public opinion, the opinions of those we don't know, can be harder to bear. "We're getting some very worrying feedback from your last meeting," is a strangely powerful thing to say to politicians. They are powerless to defend themselves against the charge. That line "I'm not running a popularity contest here" is never true in politics.

The correct administration of paranoia will reduce a person's confidence in their own judgment to the point where they will rely on your approval to proceed. Only those who enjoy administering this approval process can enter the kingdom of power.

We see this in our social lives as well ("I really had to stand up for you the other night, but I think I won in the end.") It is observable in office politics: "You didn't make a very good impression on the client but I managed to smooth it over." These are all good and useful indications to back out of the relationship as quietly as you can, or cauterise it if you can't (that has dangers of its own). You are dealing with someone who has political ambitions, someone who wishes to operate on you, to have power over you, to manipulate your well-being. Send their contact details to the political party of your choice (they may be tempted to go into public life, where you will be confident their end will be messy).

But this is dangerous, it can get out of hand. Paranoia falls into the good servant, poor master category. When it runs riot, you come to believe your telephones are tapped and that listening devices are everywhere. Winston wouldn't start his last caucus before announcing the coalition until a satellite dish on a building two hundred yards away was removed. He felt it might be a device that could pick up the vibrations from the window glass. He may have been right. Paranoids have enemies. An interesting story in the *Goss* showed that his fears might not have been unfounded.

> A former SIS agent has passed the *Goss* an intriguing piece of information. In the newspaper reports of the leaked AUSTEYES intelligence paper it said: "His [the Treasurer's] Maori agenda could prompt him to push for a more active South Pacific role; he has spoken in private of competing with Australia for influence in the region."
>
> Spot the giveaway?
>
> If Winston had been heard talking to friends in a bar, our source says, the writer would have described it as "exercising his opinion among colleagues".
>
> "Speaking in private" is intelligence jargon for information gathered from an electronic intercept: the implication is that the Treasurer was bugged.

> Now this takes a hitherto comical debacle to a new level. The SIS does not pass on information about New Zealand nationals to overseas interests so we might deduce that Australians, working out of their embassy here – are spying on our politicians.
> The information is probably being fed back into the US pool as part of their ANZUS deal.
> It would prove to be an even greater scandal if the chief political officer at the Australian Embassy didn't know which of his officers was responsible.

• *Compound vision.* Flies have an ability to see from many different angles, it's a function of the physiology of their eyes. Preb can pick up a problem as if it were a many-sided object – and look at it from every angle. This is an unusual talent and leads to unusual lines of action.

The Winebox enquiry has reported. Winston's spin is that he will appeal because the Commissioner has botched the job. The correct response is not to howl him down but the opposite. "If you won't apologise and accept the judgment – then you must do exactly that, Winston. Appeal – and quickly because everyone wants the matter settled. So table the documents you say you've been sitting on for the last six months. Let's settle it once and for all. We'll help you pay!"

This has the virtue of dragging Peters through the consequences of rhetoric and allowing the story to continue in the public arena.

Similarly, when the Serious Fraud Office cleared Tuku Morgan of fraud, Prebble wrote to Tau Henare saying, "As no fraud has been uncovered, you should reinstate the funding for Aotearoa Television." (Let's see them argue that through Parliament.)

• *Double think.* The ability to hold completely contradictory ideas in your head is an obvious requirement. If you can't ride two horses at once you shouldn't be in the circus.

• *Have a cosh in your pocket.* We frequently practise politics in our private lives, to preserve or improve our position, to undermine our rivals, to get our own way. Whenever we do or say something and hope for the opposite result from the obvious – that's politics in action.

One of my oldest female friends – that is, the one I've known for longest – has the sharpest tongue in the world. Not only is she cruel but has both wit and insight. After a cask of wine she can start an inventory of your inadequacies and it's like sitting on a bacon slicer. The only way to stop her is to have an all-purpose insult you can produce, like a cosh, and hit her with: "It's such a shame, isn't it, Amelia, that adultery's never been an option for *you*." This is politics on a personal level. Politicians usually have this wariness about themselves. In every conversation with a stranger an Amelia might emerge.

It's the threat of more to come that improves people's future behaviour.

• *Economy.* You can exhaust yourself arguing policy with everyone you meet, nitwits included. Politicians never get into an argument if they can avoid it. And the good ones never win an argument by more than they have to.

Some people will grip their fork as hard as their knife when cutting steak. Even though the fork isn't doing the work, you can see knuckles whitening – this is not economical.

• *Brains.* Yes, these are useful, despite what the satirists say. Indeed, under MMP where commando actions are more the norm than the trench warfare of the previous system, brains may be said to be vital. Forwards once only had to be able to run with a man on their backs – now they need all those passing and handling skills.

However, brains can be overrated, and cunning is more important. Politics is not governed by plans or strategies. The rolling maul theory of life prevails.

• *Swearing*. Swearing is an error. Male politicians use it as a bonding practice in a display of false confidence. One will say something coarse and expect you to respond shortly afterwards. If you don't respond the initiator feels uncomfortable.

Swearing is a sign not of a small vocabulary, but of egotism. You characterise someone with one of those short words that can be so useful. Your listeners know almost nothing more than they did. You should be saying: "The man a pale embodiment of the First Law of Darkness: he accuses others of untrustworthiness, disloyalty to the party, of criticising his colleagues to the media, and of promoting himself at the expense of the party." But all you say is: "He's a ❋◆■▼!"

The attention has switched from this object of your contempt to your feelings about this object of your contempt. Your audience knows nothing new except you don't like him.

• *Cunning*. One of Act's more talented managers had a very persuasive manner. We watched him operating over a period, particularly on those close to us, and we made a study of how he was able to effect his ideas and strategies and desires almost without seeming to do so.

In a run of friendly, appreciative and complimentary remarks about a person he'd place a burr which would lodge in his listeners' minds. Viz: "That guy's so funny – Talent? *Huge* – his stories about London just had us *on* the floor. He used to hang out in London with Richard Burton and Richard Harris – in fact they taught him to drink (something he ought to watch, I started to think about three a.m. last night when he opened the *third* bottle of whisky). But he told us *why* Richard Harris is known as the Man Called Horse. Apparently, during the making of the film . . . "

So when the appropriate moment came maybe months later, he was able to activate the knowledge (which we knew without knowing how we knew it) that our talented friend had a drink problem. Had the manager just told us his gossip straight we would have evaluated it on its merits. The sleight of hand that put the data into our minds was crucial to our acceptance of it

The praise is the vital part of the presentation. Praise says: "I have looked at this individual from many angles and weighted the good and the bad. My verdict is objective, erring perhaps on the side of charity, but I'm not going to apologise for that because it's just the kind of guy I am."

At his peak he had inseminated the whole office – he had planted these seeds about all of us in everyone's minds. He could awaken this knowledge with a look, a wink, even an arch note in his voice which was privately coded for greatest effect. Occasionally the victim would become aware that there was a private joke going on – and that everyone must have been talking about them behind their back.

This principle crosses a number of the Laws of Darkness concerning friends, paranoia and saying the opposite of what you mean.

Rodney Hide's final solution (having tried everything else) was a frontal assault and there is rarely any excuse for a frontal assault. It embarrasses everyone around you, it divides the company, it demands people choose sides (it's actually very bad manners), and it doesn't work. "I consider (this person) to be a liar and a cheat," he said to a meeting of the quarterdeck officers, "and I can't work with him."

In the shocked silence that followed, the object of the assault sighed, and gently started to praise Rodney; he enumerated Rodney's fine qualities, laid out the stress the poor fellow was soldiering under, pled with him again to take a holiday, and in eight minutes had persuaded everyone present – without ever mentioning it – that Rodney had gone completely bonkers. A genuinely masterly performance.

Cunning comes in many shades and some of it can be relatively benign – for instance, when confined to promoting your own, well-defined interests. Jim Bolger has more of this than he is given credit for. His image conceals his operating practice very effectively. In fact, so effective is it that the only examples I know of myself are all in the public domain. For instance, he defused the Winebox by ordering an enquiry – not to find out whether tax evasion had occurred, but whether there had been a conspiracy of public servants to conceal tax evasion (a far harder thing to prove). The Todd Taskforce was also given a very cunning frame of reference (its title). And he alone in Parliament has discerned the importance of the millenium. He's on the Millennium Board, with his right-hand man and ex-speech writer David Beatson chairing it. The budget has allocated substantial funding for it, and in two years' time Jim Bolger will be the public figure identified with leadership in the new century.

Vision, integrity, decency, kindness. These admirable qualities can be used in the obvious way.

3

Why they do the opposite?

AT THE beginning of this book, our peculiar history of politics was laid out showing how parties have offered one thing in opposition and delivered the opposite in government. It has happened too regularly to be accidental; it's so purposeful it is probably an integral part of the political culture. The tendency is true of individuals as much as parties. The deceptions go so deep they may be fundamental.

When the current coalition was announced many were surprised that the two leaders who had demonised each other were now in partnership. One was the embodiment of an evil government and the other would cause the wholesale collapse of the New Zealand economy.

Jim Bolger explained the seeming contradiction between what they'd said and what they'd done with the words: "That was just election rhetoric" – a frankness I found rather shocking, I have to say. We all sort of knew we couldn't believe what politicians said, but to have it confirmed straight from the old war-horse's mouth adds a new dimension to public cynicism. Is there nothing they expect us to believe? Will Jenny Shipley tell us in a few years that privatising pensions is a good thing after all? Will Helen Clark declare that lower tax rates benefit workers? Will Winston tell us that big business is actually quite responsible in paying its tax?

Anything is possible. But in the wide field of flip-flops, reversed stances and policy scams, consider the following:

• Jim Anderton started his political career as an anti-union campaigner. When he failed to get the card vote abolished at party conference he walked out of the hall never to return while Kirk was alive. The fact that they were bitter towards each other is a great testament to Jim Anderton's raw political ability (he now sports Norm Kirk's portrait on his wall as a credential).

• Muldoon started as a vigorous right-winger, probably in reaction to Holyoake's refusal to put him in the cabinet along with the other Young Turks.

• Consider too that David Lange's support for nuclear-free New Zealand was very contingent until he made such a success of it at Oxford.

• Roger Douglas' book *There's Got to Be a Better Way* advocates the government establish 16 carpet factories in the United States.

• Jim Bolger voted against the Reserve Bank Act – and not, I think, just as an oppositional flourish. We won't harp on about the no ifs, ands, buts of his undertaking to abolish the surcharge.

• Jenny Shipley, despite her reputation as a right-winger in practice and in principle, argues against privatising pensions ("Privatising pensions? But Jenny, you say that like it's a bad thing!")

To say that MPs are dishonest may or may not be true but it's not a useful way of thinking about them. Politicians occupy territory that suits them; and that depends where everywhere else has set up their position. But there is a more intractable problem built into the system. Very often, they say one thing and do another not through a lack of moral fibre – but because they are simply unable to know whether they are telling the truth or not.

In opposition it largely doesn't matter what they say so they are careless of consequences. They can demand more generous levels of benefits *and* lower interest rates for mortgage holders. They demand tariff protection for shoe manufacturers *and* cheaper shoes for children.They call for a lower dollar *and* lower inflation, higher taxes *and* higher employment – and the fact that these things are mutually exclusive is never exposed unless they get elected.

It's built into the oppositional system. During the election campaign, little Deb Morris fulminates about New Zealand's youth suicides. She becomes the Minister for Youth, and among her first statements is a defence of the country's record on youth suicide.

And if you flashed the clock back to different dates you would see everyone saying the opposite of what they are saying now. Winston (whose defence of our economic performance is now a champion's) would be denouncing the government for reckless mismanagement, Jim Bolger would be denouncing policies of deregulation, Helen would be denouncing the recovery, and only Jim Anderton would be saying the same, denouncing everyone.

To some extent it's a mystery. Why does Jack Elder turn up as a minister and start defending the official version of the last five years? Why doesn't he keep up his line of attack? Why doesn't he cry: "The problem still exists! I won't rest until it's fixed!"

Why don't they turn the heat up on the bureaucracy? The reality is they've suddenly switched team, they have a new master. They turn their face from their colleagues and their manifesto to concentrate single-mindedly on the immediate problem: the departments they've been given to run. Suddenly they've become far more of a mouthpiece for their officials than they ever thought possible.

From opposition to government your perspective changes completely. It does the full u-turn. You've been talking the economy down to damage the government, now you start talking it up (you want to own the success, and to be the bearer of good news).

In government you are confronted with a sudden, quite serious problem. It's one of reality, or at least a more complex and demanding reality. You suddenly have to live with consequences. In opposition there are no consequences of your proposals (they're never going to be adopted, you can say what your voters like to hear). But as the government you go into your first post-election briefing with the Treasury and very often come out with their heads facing the other way (we've seen this effect in films).

Treasury's irresistible in the same way your bank manager is. They know about the getting and spending part of life. Idealism, rhetoric and new ideas quickly break on the rock of those budget figures.

I noticed this effect in my small capacity. Coming in from overseas, my view was that tourism was an undignified way for a country to make its living. (Left-wing politicians know some of us feel like this and so talk about "the shame of being reduced to waiters in our own country.") But you move into the fringes of public policy and you are confronted with the budget that shows how important tourism is to its balance immediately you want any possible increase in waiters, restaurants, bus boys and bell boys.

It's a similar thing with forestry: those silent settlers look awful, have a miserable effect on country communities and change the weather for the worse. If, however, you are only considering the balance sheet, you couldn't get enough of them.

But policy isn't politicians' strong point. Politicians are a very different animal from public policy writers. When politicians advocate a policy they are at best being frank about their feelings. Compulsory unionism or privatisation of superannuation, or a declining abatement regime or increasing subsidies for the shoe-manufacturing industry (or the other million details we can't be bothered thinking about) have a variety of things to be said for and against them, but unless they're approached in an ideologically coherent way you get a dog's breakfast at the other end.

What distinguishes Roger Douglas and Richard Prebble is that they can think conceptually. MPs think anecdotally, therefore they're busy all the time, because every new example needs individual attention.

At the other end of the spectrum, Simon Upton can think conceptually but can't act on his conclusions. His ability to implement what he thinks is not of the first division – unless he has conceived it his duty to take the skin off a rice pudding. The health reforms were his first and only serious challenge. He took his chief selling principle from the example of GST.

In that instance, the government persuaded the accountants that gst was a good idea. They believed (and Simon Upton consequently believed) that what the professionals believed – accountants in the first instance and doctors in the second – the public would shortly believe. They were correct in both cases.

But the deepest problem of all is one of the limits of

knowledge. You set out with a motive, a purpose, a policy (all good) and when you achieve your ends the effect is just as likely to be very bad. You need to be a philosopher, a mass psychologist, a theologian big in economics to predict the probable contradictions in your proposals.

Reality is, it's impossible to predict the consequences of your policies. Our purposes defeat us all the time.

In the Middle Ages, a don at Magdalen College, Oxford, became outraged when a stone-mason carved a gargoyle outside his window as a caricature of himself. The don made representation and the mason was required to deface his work. He did this by hollowing out the cheeks and eye sockets until the thing became a ghastly caricature of a cadaver. The don, for the next fifty years, worked away in his room. And as the years passed, his cheeks wasted and shrivelled, his eyes sank into his head, and he inexorably grew more and more like the gargoyle. When the resemblance was again exact – he died.

This is the Law of Unintended Consequences and it constantly trips us up. This cruel law subverts most human endeavour. The unintended consequence of putting your house on the market, for instance, is to lower the price of houses.

• You provoke a currency crisis to castrate the incoming government – it allows them to dismantle your life's work.

• You build a motorway round London to relieve traffic flow – it creates the single largest congestion-site in the country.

• You run to escape predators – your twinkling ankles encourage them to chase you.

• You vote for MMP to have more control over politicians – you end up with far less.

• You push money into the economy to prime the pump and get things moving – you get stagnation and inflation.

• You create a welfare state to relieve hardship and poverty –

you create a whole class of state dependants some of whom will never work again.

But let's not be too snooty about politicians' delinquencies. Most of us have promised at some point to love and honour someone for the rest of our lives and a good half of us have done no such thing.

4

Politicians need servants

SO NOW we know something of what politicians are like, but when they are dressed in the trappings of office we are too blinded by their ordinary glamour to see what they really are. However, a politician without position is naked. The essentials are shockingly visible – the essentials consisting of whether they have power in their nature, whether they deserve it, whether they'd be able to handle it if they had it. Some clearly do have the talent for it, some clearly might grow into it, others might cope if it were thrust upon them but certainly couldn't win it for themselves – and others again are so retiring they don't even want to appear in the newspaper.

Act, being a broad-based party, had examples of all these types.

In those early days, the party's unemployed politicians came in and out of an office where staff were thoroughly preoccupied with their own concerns – publishing pamphlets, assembling data, stuffing envelopes, and talking on the telephone (it was a communications business after all).

When Preb came into this melee to join Act as leader he didn't immediately display 'the action of the tiger'. In those early days his functioning was actually quite limited. This was partly because Act at that time had a very strong corporate culture which outsiders didn't always adjust to quickly. The culture had been developed by following a variety of management styles (voodoo priests, totalitarian madmen and spiteful anarchists had all made their contribution to the manual). A volunteer once told me they had paused in a doorway and shivered. "I thought I heard a voice whispering *get ooout!*" they said to me, in reference to that film about the house in Amityville. The staff were always resigning, or threatening to resign but not going; there was a fist fight; there were nerves stretched like piano wires; there were closed doors and glass walls – an admirable setting for the administration of paranoia. This was the office which Preb's sang froid described as typical of political parties.

The fact was that Preb was out of his depth. Not that the water was too deep, far from it; the water where we were floundering was too shallow for him. He was a big, deep-sea creature; he needed some electoral tide to take him out into the main. This is more obvious now that he's in Parliament where he is clearly in his element, his natural habitat.

But because political offices are political rather than administrative it was often quite difficult getting ordinary office functions done. Difficult tasks weren't launching a superannuation policy, it was getting your typing corrected.

The task of working with politicians is more difficult than working with other more results-based executives. Everything is so much more up for grabs; everyone has an opinion, and because it's politics, everyone's opinions seemed to matter more, whatever they were. The person who was stuffing the envelopes might have the view that the party ought to coalesce with National in return for a cabinet seat. "But that's just stupid!" someone else would say.

"Possibly," responded one of the migrant professionals. "But there are a lot of stupid people out there, and they've all got a vote."

As we said earlier, mood and confidence, ideas and rhetoric were all we had to go on.

Politicians have the instincts and energies of creative types in advertising agencies combined with polemical skills and reserves of bombast. Even if they are not successful politicians they carry the conviction that they are the most important person in the room. But despite their confidence and capabilities, politicians need servants; they need people who have drunk deep of the cup of service and who will enthusiastically subordinate themselves to the purpose represented by their politicians. You probably have to be English to read this without feeling uneasy. It's a very un-New Zealand idea which came from a very un-New Zealand source, a book by Lord McAlpine called *The Servant*.

It's a book in a style and manner drawn from Machiavelli's *The Prince* written to explain and illustrate the "grandeur of service" (he was Mrs Thatcher's personal assistant, as well as Treasurer of the Conservative Party for some years).

He draws an interesting distinction between the Servant and the intelligent subordinate.

> It is beyond the capacity of the intelligent subordinate to carry out instructions without having his own thoughts about them. The Servant does not want to have to explain his plans, for this

> will lead to a series of debates and take too long. The Servant has to exercise much patience in the work he does, and none of it should be wasted on explanations. Even if the Servant has explained the plan and debated it with an intelligent subordinate, he is still likely to change the plan, making it a worse disaster than he already has.
>
> How does the Servant treat the intelligent subordinate who has done this? The Servant explains his mistake, apologising for the error of not informing the intelligent subordinate, claiming to have forgotten, and then congratulates him. Thus the Servant will have rebuked the intelligent subordinate, while also having displayed that human weakness which some confuse with humanity. In time, perhaps, the subordinate may become intelligent enough to obey without question.

I'd only read a review of this little book but looked at it more closely when working for Bolger. A Servant, in McAlpine's terms, demands a Prince and an Idea. "The Prince, the Idea and the Servant are the three legs of a stool; without any one of them the stool will topple; each one is as important as the other and each has its own distinct function."

In the second year after Bolger's first victory his popularity was lower than a prime minister's had ever been. In those days, Bolger was Prince-like and he had an Idea. The Idea was a simple one but difficult to keep to. It was an idea of tenacity, courage, endurance: while the economy was proclaimed dead by a wide variety of commentators, killed by the Reserve Bank Act, the Employment Contracts Act, the benefit cuts, his Idea was to stand by these last policy planks of Rogernomics and tough it out until the recovery came. Success is more difficult to deal with than adversity, and this was made clear when the Idea which had survived the recession didn't survive the recovery.

The Prime Minister's office finds it easy to attract capable and intelligent subordinates as well as Servants. That's one of the advantages of power. In fledgling parties, far from the centre of government, the ability to attract or create Servants was scarce. However, intelligent subordinates were everywhere.

If it's not obvious how central the pursuit of power is to ordinary members of the public, neither is it clear to the peculiar members of the public wanting to become politicians. Among all the many factions that, like crazy paving, constituted the organisation there were two groupings that held diametrically opposite views.

One faction wanted to launch the party, get out into the broad constituency and start campaigning for an election win.

The other, more conservative school of thought in the party held that

• Act should not be a political party at all, but a think tank.

• that having become a political party it shouldn't launch its policy platform until six weeks before the election.

• that having launched its policy it shouldn't field candidates.

• that, having fielded candidates who had been elected, it should coalesce with National as soon as possible, following the United example (well, it worked for them).

This school of thought is based on a reluctance to engage in the practice of vile politics; it's a policy-based vision proposed by people who have ideas about things but don't want the responsibility of seeing them put into practice (failure has a high price, after all). But experience tells us that ideas are the easy part – everybody has ideas; it's the action that's difficult.

Unfortunately we had very little relevant experience in the party: only Roger had been in opposition before, and very few of us had been involved in a start-up of anything, let alone something as difficult, as delicate, as fractious as a political party. Start-ups are very different from running existing organisations.

Starting up is always hard – starting a political party to answer questions no-one was asking was a new order of hardness.

It was a very shocking experience for the team to work so hard, to write so much, to create so much innovative policy, to have staff sign so many confidentiality agreements, to release the policy in a fanfare and to get nothing more than a picture in the paper and five hundred words of colour-copy. I am convinced that if we'd left a confidential copy in our trash and got the Coalition for the Unemployed to discover it and leak it as *Roger Douglas' secret agenda!* we would have got more value for money.

As soon as we launched, support faltered. The six full-page advertisements that followed the launch ("As the media didn't print our policy we have to put it on public record") saw support start its leisurely slide from 4.7 per cent to around one per cent (though in fairness it was some sort of achievement that deserves recording that the support never went negative).

The mystery of public opinion we never solved. Maybe it's not a problem that can be cracked. There isn't a rule you can apply. It's elusive and irrational and inspirational, and like any mob emotion transmits itself in a subconscious way from mind to mind. At a charity ball once, I saw the balloons were released onto the dance floor; people started stamping on them. When half were burst, someone tapped their balloon into the air; at once everyone stopped stamping balloons and started tapping them upwards. Like fads running through playgrounds, ideas, attitudes, feelings run through society, and their progress is so powerful it's hard to divert them. Politicians do what they can to ride them, but it's not easy even to find them. And it's almost impossible to start them.

The only way to galvanise opinion we could think of initially was through media advertising. This was considered to be an essential part of the party launch, and commonsense, letting us down again, assumed it must be so.

The trouble is that not many advertising consultants understand the peculiar business of politics. For instance they frequently say, "Politics is no different from selling baked beans." This is an infallible indicator that the agency is barking up the wrong tree. Baked beans are well-known, consistently manufactured, reliable in quality, predictable, and they are widely agreed to be good for you. None of these qualities applies to politicians.

For their part, advertising agencies don't much like dealing with political parties. Politicians are always changing their minds, they never agree to anything, they're rotten payers and even the ones who know what they want don't know what they want, and everyone in the client's office has an opinion – especially the stupid ones. Also, if the party doesn't get into government the agency fears that they won't be considered for lucrative government contracts to publicise road safety, public health and accident compensation.

Agencies, on the other hand, fail to recognise that advertising combines all the things voters most dislike about politics and about advertising – slick, costly, boastful and almost certainly untrue.

I had a theory of communications which pointed the way to a new Jerusalem of communicating public policy. We suffer from information overload (I didn't buy Sky because I'd seen an international weather report: there was light rain in central Africa). Feeling therefore that people no longer read anything, I developed techniques that used pictures and headlines to illustrate complex ideas. There had been a well-received pamphlet for the government explaining the trade-weighted index and the increase in net public debt in this way. Sensing a quickening of interest in my readers, let me expand on this. The debt image showed two versions of the same idea: a man with a monkey on his back in 1972 and the same man with a gorilla on his back in 1992. This suggested that debt had increased over the period.

The trade-weighted index was represented by two boats side by side – a broad tanker and a dinghy. The arc of swing of the two masts was represented by dotted lines. The caption said: the same wave that moves them a little moves us a lot.

Similarly, the superannuation brochures attempted to show a complex and rather boring proposition in engaging pictures. One showed a disgruntled man being handed coins for his superannuation; when you opened the brochure, a reveal changed the man's expression to a smile and piles of notes being given to him. Pictures and headlines, pictures and headlines, that was my constant cry.

The irony was that the only really effective political communication that came out of that period consisted of two books and eighty thousand words of prose. *I've been thinking* repositioned Prebble from Mad Dog to thoughtful pragmatist, and *My Journey* turned Donna Awatere Huata from Maori radical to contender for Mother of the Nation. Through the mystery of public opinion, these two books stayed at the top of the best-seller lists for three months and between them, sold forty thousand copies over the counters.

But while nobody knows what's going on, and the maul thunders on, accomplished professionals with their disciplines and strategies aren't the best advisers for politicians. For instance, we were all surprised to notice that the Quigley Party was suddenly formed two weeks before the election. Derek, who was standing as a list candidate, took the advice of very experienced advertising people, and published his election billboard on the North Shore. It consisted of a very large picture of himself and a series of statements – INTEGRITY, HONESTY, GENTLEMANLINESS, from memory. They had read the research and concluded that Derek had a larger personal following on the North Shore than had Act; the plan was to establish himself as the candidate and then convert the votes in the following week by adding the Act logo. That this strategy didn't work as well as it was hoped was clear from the electoral returns. There had been a very high personal vote and very low party vote in the North Shore (rather the opposite of what the mechanics of MMP demand). It may have been the fault of the logo which, when added, was no larger than a man's hand and functionally invisible. The Client's Complaint in advertising is traditionally, "Make the logo larger!" – but not, alas, in this case.

Towards the election we spent a serious little sum of money on a tag line, the line that sums it all up, the line you campaign on. This is the line that captures the essence of the proposition, it's what we want people to feel when they see the word "Act".

A very fine pair of advertising creatives – probably among the half dozen best in the country, probably the pair that have won more awards than anyone else in the industry – came up with the line:

If you're mad, vote Act.

I have to say that this line will be news to most of the hierarchy because I didn't dare present it. *If you're WHAT? Do WHAT?*

As a position for a party with an unusual and dashing policy agenda trying to pitch itself in the mainstream this wasn't quite the impression we wanted to make. We had always suffered from the difficulty of getting anyone serious to say pleasant things about us. Even the staff were reluctant to sport the *Roger Douglas for Prime Minister* bumper stickers that had been manufactured. But, as I say, these really were the best creative people in New Zealand.

Jeremy Taine (who'd had enough by that stage) wrote some very graceful press ads, the best of which went: *It's no wonder that our superannuation scheme was developed by a man called Rob.*

And there was an amusing series for the *National Business Review* in which the headlines were written in Albanian; a small translation showed them saying: "What is the correct price for a kilogramme of galvanised nails? Ask the appropriate minister." But by this time advertising had cost so much and done so little we didn't publish anything significant.

In fact, any impression we made on the public was not through advertising at all, and all the money spent on it was more or less wasted. Our major advantage (funding) turned out to be a hindrance – in the same way as English rugby has very large locks available to them so the selectors feel obliged to use them whether or not it's a good idea.

When Richard Griffin went to the Prime Minister's Office his reaction became famous. He repeated with a mixture of escalating amusement, exasperation and stretched credulity: "*There is no plan!*"

But it's one of the first principles of politics (and particularly visible in the formation of new parties): no-one knows what's going on. Politics is enlivened and made interesting by strategies, plans, plots, but it is not driven by them. Politics is a rolling maul, where you are more conscious of the people to your left and right than you are of the ball; you aren't sure, either, exactly which direction the line is, but the only imperative is to keep moving.

In Act's first year the rolling maul was particularly intense. In retrospect, but only in retrospect, it was quite funny. The place was crawling with communications professionals, and all of us understood through long years in the industry the importance of clarity and brand identity and firm positioning.

In six months, therefore, the party adopted half a dozen different positions: variously, the Commonsense party, the Anti-Government Waste party, the Free Enterprise party, the Superannuation party, the Tough Love party, the Save You From The Alliance party, and finally, the Future Party. (Mike Moore said: "Act is the party of the future. It will always be the party of the future," and it sounded such an original line we wondered where he'd got it from.)

The name of the manifesto was decided: *Commonsense for a change* (compulsory superannuation, universal education vouchers, zero income tax – you know, commonsense things).

A management consultant was hired to get a coherent programme in place. The first brief they were given was the most cunning: let's explore the possibility, they thought, of redefining success. The idea was to say Act would have achieved its goals if it could get its policies and principles accepted rather than politicians into Parliament. It was like one of those educationally progressive games you play where there are no losers. In fact, under that definition, Act would now be the most successful party in Parliament. Most speeches coming out of the Coalition (and, interestingly, out of the Blair government in Britain) are making Act-style noises – but in practical terms nothing that you'd notice is actually happening. And that's the difference between having the influence on what politicians say and having power over what politicians do.

But it was an altogether more comfortable goal: success would be ongoing, and there would be no defeat. The Servants – or the servants, for none of us were worthy of being capitalised – had got out of hand.

Essentially no-one could decide what the party was, and the polls were reflecting that with a rating of one per cent support.

Roger Douglas, exasperated at the failure to communicate the vision, felt certain that all we had to do was put one proposition to the country: Why would you vote to be poor?

But it was becoming clear that it didn't matter much what was said; the problem was different in kind. And it wasn't just that Act was providing the answers to questions no-one was asking. We were failing to make a crucial connection with the public.

The view I came to (but only after all else had failed) was that Act was a political party or nothing, and proceeding from that, the point of a political party was the politicians. Everything else – the advertising, the membership, the public relations drive – these were all secondary to the politicians' being the heroes of the organisation. There was no message without a messenger. The public weren't listening to what we said, they were looking at who we were. At this point, logic suggested that if we could get Ruth Richardson and Richard Prebble to join Roger Douglas in a triumvirate we wouldn't have to say anything at all about what the party was about. The public would look at those three finance ministers and say, "*I* get it! You're one of *those* parties!"

While this idea was as impractical as any, it had the rather useless virtue of being correct in principle. The lesson underlying it was that our politicians were our only real asset and that the office should be the groundcrew servicing them, the fighter pilots.

If politicians were important they certainly weren't made to feel so. Political offices are intensely political, and there was a pronounced reluctance to mythologise our heroes (admittedly this is hard when they don't want to be mythologised, but again, as we know, politicians can't display naked ambition, it doesn't work that way).

We had fallen victim to politics' first temptation: everyone had delusions of grandeur. So the advertising people thought advertising was the most important thing about Act and would impel the message into the hearts and minds of the voting public. The researchers thought they could characterise our constituency and reveal their hot buttons so they could be played like a pianola. Naturally enough, the computer people thought the demographic databases would reveal everything; the membership people thought the membership was most important. The membership would take our interesting message in pyramid teams through the country in three million face-to-faces; and most of the ten managers, with every justification, thought the management was the critical element in the equation.

Everyone had a strategy in their bottom drawer, and several were presented to the party. One or two were enthusiastically approved and endorsed, but nothing ever came of them. The other surprising characteristic of all the activity was that nothing much ever happened. Advertisements never got tested, campaigns never ran, computer programmes never got finished, teams never got formed, letters never got written (we took two months to get a direct-mail letter to the printer), and politicians never left their party to come and join us, not even Jack Elder who was desperately unhappy in Labour. The achievements in the party came from individuals or small, unofficial teams working on their own to build membership, or write and publish books, or run a media campaign.

For instance, a piece of publicity comes in with yet another typeface. This time it's been commissioned by one of the ten chief executives. The typeface has been specially chosen by a typographic consultant. It looks like a font that would have been futuristic forty years ago; it's a thin, rounded sans serif that looked weak as well as pedestrian. "Precisely because Act is seen as a futuristic party with a highly technical platform it should present its communications in a comforting manner with a traditional serif face," I said. "Computer companies have discerned this and that's why" (here I leafed through a computer magazine) "all major computer companies advertise their products with traditional serif faces."

"Simon," the chief executive said, "do you have *any* idea what you're talking about?"

Politics needs as many ancillary services as it can afford to buy but only to serve the politicians' direct needs. A party can do without research (the Alliance), without members (New Zealand First), without advertising (all of them) but no party can exist without politicians (which is why the Liberal Party doesn't exist any more).

Going a further step, the leadership was even more important than the rest of the caucus. I knew it was true that when the media wanted to talk to the Alliance they would only accept Jim Anderton on air; if they couldn't get him they wouldn't do the story. The leader embodied the party; only the leader had the shared body of experience with the viewers and listeners. If we had no leader we had nothing.

As Roger had announced he wouldn't stand for Parliament let alone for leader we were a headless animal (and one without much of a body either). But having identified the problem, the solution was very elusive. Who could lead Act? Who could be the Lange character that could establish that mysterious connection with the public and have our constituency's hopes and fears invested in their success?

Craig Heatley had what the the transvestite vampire in the *Rocky Horror Show* called "a certain naive charm" in political terms. He was new, fresh, intelligent, interesting, decent, and very credible. His only lack was that he knew nothing about Parliament (though that didn't bother us). More seriously, leading a political party was the last thing he wanted to do.

David Walden, one of the ten chief executives, certainly had many political skills and useful instincts, if they could be asserted in public. He wasn't keen either. Peter Blake's name was mentioned, though quite why was never made clear. Rosanne Meo was mooted and well thought of (though I don't think she thought as well of us as we of her). Someone outside the organisation felt he'd cracked the leadership with a brilliant, brilliant suggestion: Dame Cath Tizard (no-one inside the organisation could be found to speak in her favour).

But Prebble was a constant presence just outside our perimeter fence, and I am pleased to say, I never seriously thought anyone else could do the job. If Roger was the architect of Rogernomics, Prebble was the chief executive, turning round those twenty-two state trading organisations from loss to profitability within a year.

But it was hard to see at that time why anyone would willingly come into the office as leader. We had a hard enough time getting volunteers to come in and stuff envelopes.

Politicians ranked as low in the hierarchy of priorities as they did in every public poll – so low in fact, that one of the ten chief executives thumped the boardroom table and said, "These are things that must be said by the leader, and if he won't say them," and he jerked his thumb towards Roger Douglas' office, "we'll get a new leader!"

It shows the power of prose, because taking McAlpine's book seriously I decided on a career of servitude, to follow politicians' instincts rather than my own and see where it would lead, and it was at that point I started be able to learn about politics.

There were two moments of great intrigue when Act connected with parliamentarians. It seemed almost certain to some of us that Act would attract half a dozen MPs and a cabinet minister – two even – to form a parliamentary party well before the last election.There were meetings between our people and their people. Pauline Gardiner came up to examine our policy (or more probably, to examine our people).

Finally, that United group of MPs decided Act was too extreme. They charted a course for the centre, for that haven, that oasis where both left and right came to refresh themselves. In fact, the centre turned out to be a waste disposal unit which swallowed them whole.

In a parallel series of negotiations, the cabinet minister Maurice Williamson had come to the very point of declaring publicly he was going to lead Act into the election. He came up for the final meeting and made it clear that he was off to see Bolger on Saturday morning to break the news to him. "But," he was asked, "what if Bolger says you can't be in Cabinet any more? What if he says you can't be in the National party any more?"

To all what-ifs he replied that he was coming to lead Act and that consequences on the other side of the fence were irrelevant.

It was beginning to look as though my $500 bet was going to enrich Owen Jennings' family. But in the event, Maurice came in on Monday to say that he'd been to see Bolger, he had the meeting, they'd talked it through and . . . he needed more time. It was clear he was a busted flush. And not only did I eventually get the cheque from Owen (which hangs in my downstairs lavatory) the decks had also been cleared to arrange the passage of Prebble back into politics.

5

The art of the spin

ONE OF Winston's great achievements was giving form to the idea that unelected officials and consultants run the country more than politicians do. Spin doctors, speech writers, policy analysts, industry liaison officials, permanent secretaries, colour consultants, image therapists – the retinues in politics are long and they have an important but not central influence on politicians. Those with a weakness for conspiracy theories will be happy to believe these well-paid officers and officials push and pull public policy out of recognition, that our elected representatives are deceived by *la trahison des clercs.* There is some evidence for this but it's not decisive.

And way out on the other edge of things, we have the unelected bureaucrats, the Treasury mandarins with their degrees and invisible careers – the clever clogs and time-servers, the arse-coverers and place-holders, the viral elements of the body politic, the creatures you'll never get rid of, they're there indefinitely, like luggage. It is also tempting to believe that these puppet-masters, far more than here-today-gone-tomorrow politicians, determine what shall be done.

Bob Jones' support for Winston – which was both financial and professional – was based on Winston's capacity to whip these unelected officials into obeying the will of the people (it didn't quite turn out like that, in the event).

Michael Wall was quite right in his diagnosis of MMP: he predicted that under the new system, of the three estates in the political establishment, two would gain in influence and one would fall. So it happened: the stars of the bureaucracy and the media are rising, and that of the politicians' is in decline.

The media perform a galvanising role in their search for and celebration of conflict. The bureaucracy, out of sight, out of mind, provides the underlying machinery that makes things happen. And then the politicians' staff determine how it shall be presented. All are competing for their preferred spin to become the conventional wisdom on any issue of the day, substantial or trivial.

What is spin? Spin is pitching a piece of neutral-looking information in such a way as to serve your cause. In sport, pitchers get a ball, they chuck it at the batsman and put a spin on the thing so that it deceives the player: the ball kicks up around the bat (in cricket), or is struck by the batsman but goes where the pitcher wants (as in baseball). An inert, neutral item, the ball, has taken on a life of its own.

In its lower form, spin can be creating original and powerful euphemisms. For instance, in Britain, heavy-drinking foreign secretary George Brown stumbled down the steps of an airplane and made a slurred and rambling speech to the media – his spin doctor explained that after a long flight the minister was "tired and emotional". Overuse has dimmed the original brilliance of this expression; it quickly became a euphemism for being shit-faced. Michael Laws' talented creation in the same arena was to keep "European hours".

Back in England, a female television journalist was discovered in full sexual embrace under some coats at a party. "We were just talking about Uganda," she spin-doctored, rather breathlessly in the event. "Ugandan discussions" quickly enriched the language.

There is, as well, the opposite of spin. An American businessman was on the radio saying: "If the government persists in its course of action we will probably withdraw from this country and set up head office elsewhere."

"Is that a threat?" the interviewer asked urgently, "Are you threatening us?" It's impossible to answer this question on air, it's a *have you stopped beating your wife* question (only General Noriega was able to answer that; he said, "No. Why?") Trade union officials are asked if they are threatening strike action, but they are too canny to answer frankly. Only bullies, psychos and criminals *threaten*.

But the businessman was a Teutonic American who was able to take the question literally and came up with the laborious but definitive: "It is not a threat. It is an affirmative expression of a business strategy." He stopped the ball in mid-air, rubbed the spin off and batted where he wanted it to go.

General Rabuka takes the prize for the least spun response to a question – it was during the military takeover of Fiji. An excited New Zealand journalist had got an exclusive interview and was quizzing him about the legal basis for the recent action. The General fudged his reply, and the journalist pounced, rather: "So what you're saying is there is *no* legal basis for what you're doing here at all?"

The General smiled his big Fijian smile and said carefully, "It is neither legal nor illegal . . . It is a *coup*, you see."

This frankness, the opposite of spin, was still in evidence a couple of years ago. An Indian journalist was questioning him pointedly about the constitutional status of ethnic Indians in Fiji. The General said: "Just because Indians are smarter than we are, and just because Indians work harder than we do does not mean they will own more than we own."

"But," the journalist asked, "is that not racist?"

"*Only insofar as it applies to Indians*," the General played his trump card triumphantly.

Michael Laws generated another marvellous piece of spin this year. In August, during the debacle surrounding associate health minister Neil Kirton being fired from the government, the newsreader announced, "Michael Laws, who himself resigned from Parliament last year on an issue of accountability . . . " And he went on to quote Michael's slant on the events in question. I was most struck by the phrase "on an issue of accountability" so redolent of integrity and high-mindedness, so beyond criticism. In fact, Michael deceived the Napier Council and misled the House of Representatives and that was the end of his parliamentary career. His brilliant spin would translate into a burglar saying he had been jailed over an issue of private property.

Just as subtle was John Delamere being reported from Waitangi during the celebrations. He was quoted on the developing Aotearoa Television scandal saying, "Tuku was ribbed mercilessly about his taste in expensive clothes . . . " (oh I *see*, it's a Maori thing, we've all been taking it too *seriously!* We've just being culturally insensitive!)

The measure of how careful public figures are, how scrutinised everything is, how *spun* everything they say is, can be gauged by the shock we feel when we hear them speaking frankly. The Australian government's security report that fell into media hands earlier this year had enormous repercussions because it said in plain language that certain South Pacific leaders were corrupt, or drunk, or hopeless. (This is hardly news.)

Unspun concepts are very dangerous though. If you have a harsh budget, for instance, it is most unwise to call it the Mother of All Budgets.

Lockwood Smith's talented press secretary came up with a couple of very useful lines: When asked if a rumour was true he'd say, "It's certainly true there's a rumour," which made it difficult for the journalist to proceed with further useful questions. And his advice for the fracas in Cafe Brava (the Treasurer was involved in a verbal attack on a young woman – "In ten years time you'll be ugly!") was for Winston's office, when questioned about the events to say, "Nothing out of the ordinary happened." Again, a stop-dead, cul-de-sac of a reply.

I managed a little amateur spin when working for Jim Bolger. A couple of things were useful, perhaps. Two conventional criticisms of Mr Bolger were that he lacked charisma and had no sense of humour. My line was that it was precisely Muldoon's charisma and Lange's sense of humour that had brought the country to the edge of bankruptcy: You say Bolger is boring and uncharismatic but he has safe hands and it has been he who brought us safely back from the brink.

Of the Winebox I said that the conditions of the early 80s were as different from today's as war time was from peace time. In war time, different standards of behaviour are acceptable; the question at issue consisted of whether the companies were simply committing the exuberant slaughter that wins you a medal in war time, or whether they had actually committed war crimes.

There were other more difficult conundrums. In a time of rising unemployment and rising crime it is difficult to deny the connection between them (remember the interview on *Holmes* when Paul demanded more employment to slow the murder rate).

You still hear the idea promulgated that in times of high unemployment ill-health, suicide and other forms of premature death increase among the poor, the elderly and Polynesians. When the call is for governments to do something about it, it sounds heartless to say that tax reductions for the better-off are the answer (to increase business confidence, employment and ultimately wages). Politicians don't care to say (or even dare to think) that by removing themselves from the equation the problem will solve itself (or what's the point of them?)

But spin is not confined to politicians. Schools are the great spin factories of the day. Apparently, Japanese school books carry a description of the Second World War that would be unfamiliar to any other nation.

In the west, the political correctness movement is a spin on history, one that casts down the arrogant dead white males with their overweening achievements and exalting almost everyone else. In this view of history we are taught how daring Polynesian navigators discovered these islands in great voyages of Pacific exploration in their canoes – while at the same time, Europe was a squalid dump of barbarism and cruelty where children were executed, workers were tortured and women suffered systematic abuse. From a politically correct viewpoint, the Pacific discoverers were in a Steven Spielberg production, full of adventure, sunshine and discreet good hair styling. Europe was a *Mad Max* kind of show, directed by Terry Gilliam and characterised mainly by mud, rags, warts, and people having their heads torn off.

Schools are not always in close touch with the world they teach about. Prebble helped one of his offspring write a school project: How the Budget is put together (he was an associate minister of finance at the time). The teacher gave them a C.

The media is always susceptible to statistical spin from talented lobbyists. AIDS activists reigned supreme for a decade. Statements such as "Extrapolating present rates of growth in the virus, by the year 1990, sixty per cent of the population will be infected" were accepted as reasonable, and indeed resulted in wide government activity – though not much change of behaviour in low-risk groups. It was clear from the beginning that the virus which travelled in a very similar way to hepatitis would follow a similar growth pattern. That is, it would be endemic in parts of Africa, and largely confined to certain specific behaviour groups in the west. This is largely the case, and while the tragedy is not alleviated by numbers, it is also true that only about a thousand New Zealanders are reported HIV positive and the disease itself is showing signs of reducing in virulence.

Be this as it may, politics is where spin is most observable, most practised, most important.

Earlier this year, the official information was clearly indicating a recession. All the stats were going the wrong way – business confidence was falling, retail sales were down, investment, economic growth were all reduced, and unemployment was on the rise again. Winston's spin was that these were *encouraging* figures (at the bottom of our economic cycle we were doing better than other countries).

Few politicians have the charm to pull off such a daring delivery (he had been denouncing the earlier recovery, with great display of passion). But as Treasurer, the spin has worked: he cannot be made to confront an imminent recession, and one that his very presence in government has caused.

Spin is to look into a Rorschach Test and construct completely different pictures from the coloured blobs. Psychologists use the test to gauge the psychological well-being of their patients. One person looks at the blobs and sees a gannet, another sees a handbag; one person sees a thundercloud, another sees a child smiling. Politicians use the same ability to create pictures in which their voters can judge their own well-being.

Ordinary people look into the Rorschach Test that constitutes the economy and see only a chaos of boring statistics. Building permits are down but retail advertising is up – what does that mean? Does the increased advertising suggest greater growth? Or are they panic selling and trying to get rid of surplus stock before the recession hits?

Spin doctors use statistics like these to conjure up an image of a gathering recession; rival spin doctors will use the same statistics to herald the beginnings of an economic boom. And graduate spin doctors, spinmeisters perhaps, can also construct a recession gathering while a boom is actually thundering forward.

Thus, at the beginning of this year, Richard Prebble looked into the business plans of a number of companies and deduced just after Christmas that there would be a recession. In none of the plans he saw was there any investment, or recruiting, no expansion planned anywhere. A couple of months later he confirmed his predictions from another unofficial indicator: freight volumes on the railways were down.

The mystery of this year's recession has been why the media have played it all down so much. While the rest of the world's stockmarkets were firing away, New Zealand was left wallowing in standing water. By August there still wasn't any sense of concern in the headlines. A poll showed that only six per cent of people thought it was a bad budget. Perhaps this was why even the dollar dropping fifteen per cent against sterling in a fortnight didn't encourage editors to think a panic could be generated: *Dollar collapses! Importers bleed! Home owners can't sell!*

In a reaction to a decline in overseas investment, the business editor of Radio New Zealand said: "Oh, I think it's just investors realising they can make a profit elsewhere," in that offhand way that suggests there's nothing untoward happening. In another mood he could have said, "Overseas investors are piling out of New Zealand as they see this country's performance sliding into mediocrity and politics returning to the marketplace. God only knows what will become of us!"

The government spin has prevailed: it's all cyclical. The most common report in the media was: "There was a small contraction in the first quarter; we'll have to wait and see whether that trend is confirmed in the second- quarter results."

But the media spin on the economy is intensely unreliable. Remember the other extreme, five years ago, while the sharemarket was doubling and unemployment was rapidly falling, Jim Anderton was able to be approvingly quoted in the press and on television saying that everything was getting very much worse, that unemployment would double by Christmas, inflation would hit fifteen per cent, and there would be zero growth (the opposite of all these things actually happened).

Jim Anderton is more consistent, of course, than those who report him. Three years ago, when confronted with a growth figure of 4.2 per cent, Jim Anderton said he doubted the economy had grown that much. "If the figure was a true 4.2 per cent growth, close to sixty thousand extra jobs would have been created during 1992-3 instead of the twenty three thousand jobs that were actually created."

Jim's a highly intelligent man and widely experienced in all matters of public policy, if not at the highest level (never been in cabinet). So why, or more accurately *how*, can such a sincere man say these things?

His reality is the political reality where you can create the world by thinking about it. More kindly, it's a question of perspective and point of view.

His constituency – and Michael Cullen's (who was predicting a two per cent growth over the same period) – had not been touched by the recovery. Property values hadn't lifted, so tilers and carpenters hadn't felt demand for their services. Understandably, if you understand these things, Jim Anderton could say what he wanted to his constituency because he was only saying what they all believe. (It's Homer Simpson's First Law of the Playground: Never say anything unless you know everyone agrees with it.)

Less clearly, but most important for the spinners of conventional wisdom, there are a number of economic forecasting agencies who supply a wide range of economic forecasts. And they are almost as partial, or as partisan, as politicians are. Because they have a specific world view they can be relied on to dramatise statistics sympathetic to that view.

The Alliance get their forecasts from BERL I believe and from Len Bayliss' Gamma Foundation. These agencies' forecasts are invariably more pessimistic than agencies who forecast for the right. Kelly Tonkin, Roger Kerr and any of the trading banks have been closer to the mark recently. Brian

Gaynor characteristically offers a picture of New Zealand's prospects informed by a Celtic melancholy.

Certainly, Jim Anderton was given the statistics that helped him successfully deny a recovery was happening for so long that by the time it was undeniable he was able to claim the economy had peaked and we were headed into another recession.

This shifting, chimerical reality is everywhere in politics. Norman Kirk was asked that perennial question "What is a New Zealander?" He replied, "Anyone who thinks they are a New Zealander," a statement that is neither true nor useful to anyone except a politician.

To illustrate how we are all caught up in this imaginative reality, how relative it all is, have a look at a news story you will recognise.

It is headlined: GAP BETWEEN RICH AND POOR WIDENS. These reports come out most years following international surveys of economic activity in the world. What does the story mean?

It can mean one or both of two quite opposite things. It depends which way you prefer to approach it. If you come from the left you major on the fact that the poor are getting relatively poorer and say: "This demonstrates that capitalism by itself will not produce a fair distribution of wealth and therefore governments have a moral duty to intervene by taxing the rich to provide services in health, education and superannuation for the poor."

If you prefer to look at it from the right you focus on a different fact and say: "The poor are getting absolutely richer, and while they are getting a lower proportion of world trade in absolute terms they are getting more trade because world trade is increasing. They are better off than if world trade was declining – their share would collapse faster than developed nations."

Notwithstanding the interpretations, the fact of the gap is better than a fact. These highly politicised pieces of information are what I call factoids, a word I have come to use in a private sense.

A factoid is better than a fact, it's a super-fact, a parafact, a factoid is the best expression of spin there is. It is a fact that appears neutral but actually carries very powerful ideological conclusions. They are organising facts. Once you have absorbed them they become part of your character. They influence your view of the world. If you can get factoid into the information economy it will combine with other facts or information to help build a conventional wisdom. Factoids are powerful enough to reorganise the flow of other information.

Factoids from different ends of the spectrum sound like these:

• The rich are getting richer and the poor are getting poorer. (*Taxation should be increased to even out inequality in the world.*)

• The rich are getting richer and the poor are getting richer (*Taxation should be reduced to make poor people richer.*)

• Incomes have risen in real terms by twenty per cent over the last generation but no-one's better off because the state has taken all the extra in higher taxes. (*Governments are insatiable.*)

• Every year, seventeen thousand children in America have their faces bitten by rats. (*Things happen that are intolerable for civilised people: governments must act.*)

• Government collects the same amount of tax when income tax is at forty per cent and twenty per cent. But at the lower rate, citizens will end up having kept three times as much money as at the higher rate. (*Lower taxes are good for economies' growth.*)

• School principals hate bulk funding. (*School principals are obstructive lefties – or alternatively, school principals are stalwart defenders of the public education system.)*

• Keynes' analysis of prices showed that the pound was worth the same in 1915 as it was in 1826. It was only when the Bank of England was nationalised that inflation really took off. (*Inflation isn't necessary for growth.*)

• Just because a contract is 150 years old doesn't make it less potent in law: Hong Kong was handed back to the Chinese when the lease ran out. (*The Treaty of Waitangi is a valid document.*)

• Eighty-five per cent of New Zealanders agreed with a compulsory private superannuation scheme until Winston Peters started proposing it. (*It's all Winston's fault.*)

• The economy was so heavily regulated in the '70s that you needed a doctor's prescription to buy margarine, and the permission of the Reserve Bank to subscribe to an overseas magazine. (*We've forgotten how deadening the effects of government regulation were.*)

• There are natural limits to economic growth. (*We must conserve natural resources by regulation. Or alternatively, the Club of Rome has been proven wholly wrong, capitalism naturally conserves resources by price mechanisms – when resources get scarce they get more expensive.*)

• New research links the Government's economic reforms with a rise in the death-rate of low-income, middle-aged New Zealanders. (*Reforming governments are systematically eliminating its opponents.*)

• The right engage in moral relativism too: they justified apartheid by a This Is Africa argument. (*They're accusing the left of their own faults.*)

Many of these factoids have the added virtue, as politicians say, of being true.

The factoid principle can be extended to book length. In prose terms, factoids become anecdotes. The author refrains from saying outright: "This made me angry," but instead tells a story that makes the audience feel angry on their behalf. We have to agree that *I've been thinking* and *My Journey* are models of their kind.

Richard Prebble tells how the Railways lost a farmer's tractor between Hamilton and Taumarunui. The department was unable or unwilling to find the tractor. Eventually the farmer followed the line himself, looking in every goods yard along the way. Eventually he found the tractor along with six wagons similarly lost.

(*One farmer with the right incentives out-performs 22,000 state employees with the wrong ones.*)

Donna's book has been able to reorganise white New Zealanders' minds about Maoridom with a number of compelling factoids.

The first was that certain Maori tribes were boisterous commercial traders. The Waikato tribes had half a dozen windmills, a fleet of ocean-going vessels exporting wheat to Australia and a market-gardening operation that supplied Auckland via a thousand carrier canoes. (*Maori were a vigorous, confident race before the Treaty was signed.*)

The second was that Maori land was alienated not by battle in the nineteenth century but by bureaucrats as recently as the 1960s. One tribe saw tree contractors planting on their ancestral lands; they followed the chain of command and found in an office in Wellington that the land had been taken by the government thirty years before but they hadn't been informed – there was no legal requirement to do so. (*The problems of grievance are not ancient history.*)

The third was a description of her visit to a state orphanage; the ex-Rhodesian superintendent was dressed in riding boots with spurs, a leather jacket, with a big bunch of keys on his leather belt. The five, six and seven-year-old children were treated as prisoners in a remand home.

"But there was something else," she says.

"Round a covered courtyard there were a series of solitary confinement cells. There were four things in the cells: an iron bed, a mattress, a potty and a loudspeaker. I saw a boy in one and I recognised him. I went forward to talk to him and a loudspeaker said, "*Move away from the cell!*" I did not do so. I found he had been in that cell for three months. No-one knew where he was. I was able to tell his mother where he was when I got out. She had been looking for him through the system ever since he disappeared." (*New Zealand had more in common with South Africa than we would ever have imagined at the time.*)

The concept of passing the cup came from one of those Kahlil Gibran aphorisms: "The artist prepares a cup whereof he does not drink himself." This ability to pass the cup, let the audience drink (or in plain language to come to a conclusion they think they have arrived at themselves) is a very important one.

The failures of the genre are, however, more entertaining. Bryan Gould's book *Goodbye to all that* is a case in point (there's a perfectly good book of that title already – there's the first mistake). The book records Gould's very successful career in Britain. It is the account of a talented, successful, ambitious, diplomatic, telegenic, athletic, charismatic New Zealander. The only trouble is that Bryan Gould wrote it himself. Far from passing the cup to his readers, Bryan drains it off himself (and, incidentally, reveals the pathology of politicians with embarrassing frankness).

Here is a collapsed version of the book:

I not only made the team but supplanted the club captain as

number one in the team.

By now I felt at the height of my powers. I had got a first. My degree was rated at that time as the second-best BCL since the war. I have always had the capacity to look positively at every situation. My lectures were a great success. There was a table tennis tournament which I won.

At Westminster I quickly made my mark. One had suddenly become a great focus of attention. Now I spoke powerfully on this issue. I would have been the first of my intake to gain such recognition.

I became quite confident in my handling of issues across the whole range of macroeconomic policy. Very few understood the issues.

He nodded thoughtfully and commented that Helmut took the same view.

I had an appreciative note from Neil Kinnock in reply. I have no doubt that this endorsement of my critique was genuine. As always I worked hard. Mine were the forensic skills and I enjoyed the cut and thrust of debate. My very focused views on economic policy meant that I could develop an expertise that few others could match. I felt myself to be at the height of my powers both personally and politically. I was well respected and widely listened to.

I had realised that if I were to make any progress in the party, I needed political friends. Tribune was, however, a great disappointment. It had changed character entirely and was now merely a vehicle for careerists.

My standing with my colleagues rose considerably, since there was no-one else in the Labour Party capable of understanding the issues. Despite the excitement of my promotion to the shadow cabinet, I was disappointed with the job I was actually offered.

> I found myself in constant demand as a spokesperson for the party in every situation. Neil's [Kinnock] confidence in me grew. We rapidly reached the point where he wanted me to do everything. I in turn formed a new respect for Neil.
>
> My own relations with my colleagues were good, although it must have been galling to them to see a newcomer attract so much attention.
>
> Neil turned to me often for advice but more particularly to undertake tasks which he feared might be too difficult for others. I topped the poll by a wide margin.
>
> For the first time, I think, Neil saw me as a potential rival. Peter was also beginning to believe his own myth. He increasingly saw himself as the fixer of party affairs and as Neil's mouthpiece.
>
> No-one dared take me on in argument since, I assume, they realised they would not get the better of it.
>
> I was even more surprised when my comments were repudiated by Neil the following day.
>
> My confidence in the prospects of national renewal received a further blow. The dreams I had harboured since childhood of a rejuvenated Britain, perhaps leading the world again as an efficient, humane and democratic post-industrial society seemed unlikely to be realised.
>
> I realised in essence I was a New world person.

"The single nastiest review I've ever read," Richard Prebble was kind enough to say, "Bryan must have been shattered by it . . . unless he thought you'd printed all the best bits?"

6

Why gossip is important

THERE are said to be six degrees of separation in the world. That is, the Vietnamese peasant knows a seed distributor who knows a tax collector in Sang Pon who knows an official in Hanoi who knows a First Secretary in the Embassy whose boss has met the Queen. But that's easy, everyone knows someone who knows someone who knows someone who knows the Queen. The real test is how many contacts does it take for your mother-in-law to know the person who does the pies at the BP station in Turangi? Studies in actuarial firms suggest that the degrees of separation in New Zealand are around 1.8 (we remember that everyone knew someone who knew someone on flight 901).

For these reasons, New Zealand's talent for gossip is unrivalled.

On one occasion a couple of English friends touring from England were scheduled to come for dinner at our house in

Hawke's Bay; I was in Auckland and couldn't get back in time. Nor did I know where the Peakes were staying, just that they were somewhere in central Hawke's Bay with someone called White. Because it was imperative I get hold of them, I called Mrs Atcheson. She said something which astonished me ("I don't know anyone called White") and then suggested I call the storeman at the dairy in Onga Onga because he knew everything and would probably be able to give me a lead. "I'm looking for a couple of English tourists who are staying somewhere in Central Hawke's Bay with someone called White, can you help at all?"

The storekeeper, unfazed by this request, reflected a country moment and said, "You wouldn't be talking about the *Peakes* would you? Middle-aged? From Dorset? They're staying with the Whites, and as a matter of fact John Peake's just pulled onto the forecourt for some petrol, do you want a word with him? Hey, John? There's a call for you!"

In this thick soup of New Zealand society where there is an almost tribal density of relation between us all, everyone is within grappling distance. The word of mouth is all-powerful. Radio Pacific talkback host Jenny Anderson once said that the real reason support for the Alliance was slumping was because the tom-toms had started beating about Jim Anderton. Stories of his relations with his family were circulating at supermarket level. It was to counter this that Jim went on *Holmes* and was given one of the most abrupt short-arm tackles ever seen on television. Anderton started talking about how marvellous the hospital staff were in caring for his son and Holmes broke in to ask him: "You say you've come on the programme to speak for your family. Why is it, Mr Anderton, that I've had your daughter on the phone to me twice today, *begging* me not to let you on?"

It made us all wince, even those with no natural sympathy for Mr Anderton.

But gossip reveals character; it is to catch a glimpse of character in action before it has been remodelled, restyled, touched up and had five pounds taken off it by staff.

For instance: around the time of the Springboks tour, the Young Nats conference was held at the Chateau. It was a period when the hotel was state-owned, and at the weekend, a fleet of black Impalas carrying politicians and their entourages to this, their country estate, their dacha, would pull up at the front door. We have forgotten now how respected politicians were in those days – how hated some were, but how much less despised they were then than they are now.

The president of the organisation, Simon Upton, might have been showing off to Muldoon who was guest speaker, but he called for 'the little Maori boy' (the chief steward) to do a whero with a broom handle for the group. As this was the year of the Springboks tour the request had an unfortunate ring. The waiter did as he was asked for Mr Upton, and took great care of him for the rest of the conference. When Mr Upton's port glass needed filling, Tommy would take it carefully to the butler's pantry and fill it with a specially fine old port, taking care first, however, to rub his substantial penis very thoroughly round the rim of the glass.

I'm not sure what this story means, or exactly why it's worth repeating, but I am very glad to know it and feel that it adds something to the glamour of this book – such is the power of gossip. Perhaps it's a parable of how powerful people, or people in positions of power, shouldn't treat waiters badly. News of their unattractive habit eventually gets out – as it has here – quite apart from the fact that there are more immediate consequences.

I made up a joke once, something I've only ever done once. "What do Eskimos get when they sit on an igloo? – Polaroids!" I told three people and forgot about it; eighteen months later the joke turned up on the Benny Hill Show. It's marvellous how news travels when people want to repeat it.

One of the creations of the new environment is the *Goss*, a gossip sheet put out by fax which has caught the mood of the new politics. The only people to hate it more than Roger Douglas are the Nats and New Zealand First (who provide the punchlines for most of the jokes).

They all dislike it for the same reason: it subverts the dignity of parliamentarians. It penetrates their cloistered world and exposes their conceits and foibles to the vulgar gaze. You park your ministerial car in a disabled space at the supermarket and it appears in the *Goss*. You register your private car with a parliamentary stamp warrant and it appears in the *Goss*. You're on a parliamentary visit to Australia and trash your hotel room and it appears in the *Goss*.

Those politicians who criticise it for triviality don't realise that triviality doesn't exist any more, not in the current political environment. They also don't realise how out of touch they are with their electorates: constituents are enraged by these trivial acts of discourtesy – and bearing in mind the Third Law, the trivial (if symbolic of a larger flaw) can be extraordinarily powerful. It may also be true there is an element of schadenfreude in the public reaction to these stories, an element of revenge; winning even a minor skirmish in the running battle between people and politicians gives the public heart.

There is a thought that those who make the laws can come to feel themselves to be above the law. There is a constant temptation for politicians to retreat into the world of privilege. British MPs take risks that betray the psychotic bedrock on which many of their careers are founded. They come to believe they exist in a level of society where the police take orders from them, inured from the normal conventions we plebs, proles and serfs abide by. The tabasco of good gossip, as it makes their eyes water, can jerk them back into a more ordinary reality.

The *Goss* also interests those who can't be bothered with politics any more because of the language the business is conducted in.

It was observed in America that elections are fought over the two ways of dealing with the economy, and that the language of politics had become the language of economics; yet most people know as much about economics as they know about imperial Roman poetry. So, asking voters to choose between these two theories of dealing with the deficit was like asking them to choose between rival translations of Catullus.

This mandarin language is alienating; most people can't speak it, most don't want to. So while the great policy battle goes on in motion so slow as to be imperceptible, the *Goss* helps the political battle scamper briskly along.

So, the *Goss* laughs at Deb Morris for putting out a ministerial press release criticising the mess round a recycling centre. While this story doesn't exactly say, "Your working with the ministry for senior citizens to devise a strategy for inter-generational harmony is a fool's errand," it does seek to undermine the point of having a minister of youth at all.

• When Neil Kirton sees his new post-ministerial office he throws a tantrum that is impressive – even by his own demanding standards – that he is reaccommodated in the Beehive. This says as much about him as his ideological commitments – and possibly more (his ideology is more likely to change than his character).

• Arthur Anae said on radio he wanted state support for the

koha he is culturally committed to distributing. That is, he wants between $200 and $1500 of public money to take to political meetings in order to give it to those who turn up.

• A ministerial offspring has a party in the minister's house while the minister is away in Italy, and the invitations are sponsored by a tobacco company.

These stories all have their role in the rich and detailed skein of MMP politics. Venal some of them may be, but then that's why people like it.

It's important to take on board that under MMP there is no such thing as trivia any more.

Under the new voting arrangements, party solidarity is less formidable than it used to be. New politicians arrive in new parties and they don't have the tribal commitment to their party – Alamein on one side of the spectrum, dear old Quig on the other, and Neil Kirton somewhere in between have all parlayed up their position by indicating they aren't to be taken for granted.

Under the old voting system there was nowhere to go, minor parties didn't exist; now the balance of power is more sensitive. One defecting Nat would throw the government into turmoil; one good scandal could bring the government down.

Trivia is significant, sometimes fiscally significant. Indeed, the government recently declared that Tuku's underwear was responsible for the recession. They didn't phrase it exactly like that but the thrust was unmistakable. They said that business confidence was down because of the attention given to "sideshows" in the coalition (underwear, hotel room trashing, a $35,000 junket to Paris, a contract given to a brother-in-law); this was why, the government declared, there was a lack of business confidence in the coalition which in turn meant the tax take would be down, and therefore the surpluses were affected and that tax cuts could be compromised next year. If Tuku's underwear can affect a three-billion-dollar surplus there is certainly no such thing as trivial gossip any more.

You would be right to be sceptical of their clever spin ("reporting political scandal is economic sabotage"): the fundamentals for the recession were in place prior to and just after the election, and they consist of a government spend-up of some billions and a Treasurer with a penchant for buying votes.

But most subtle is the preparing of the ground, when people don't realise what you are even doing. The planting of a seed that will grow. It was the lesson taught by the most cunning of our chief executives (the learning of which nearly put us in a rest home).

Ruth Laugesen once said that she was reluctantly admiring of the powerful propaganda tool the *Goss* was. "You report that Winston hasn't had anything to do with the Budget papers and twenty-four hours later it's the conventional wisdom round the place. It's deplorable, but amazingly effective."

The *Goss* reported that Winston is lazy, he hasn't got a grasp of economics and that he drinks too much. This was later countered by his side planting stories about his twenty-five meetings a day and punishing workload, but the European hours have probably taken precedence (if the AUSTEYES briefing paper was anything to go by). Nowadays the *Goss* (which is nothing if not scrupulously fair) is reporting that Winston seems more in command of his brief than he has been and is a passable imitation of a treasurer.

7

Why sex is important

THERE are certain personal details about public figures which are of legitimate interest. You could argue that MPs' financial circumstances have a bearing on what they'll do: how dependent, for instance, are they on their pretty reasonable salaries? Whose mortgage depends on full-term government? So who's *definitely* not going to bring the government down?

Less extreme, we should certainly have a register of MPs' interests listing directorships and contracts with interest groups.

But Richard Griffin expresses the general view when he says that a public figure's private life, particularly in matters of sex, is irrelevant to their public duties. This magnanimous attitude would almost certainly be true of the prominent male interviewer who is said to have an extensive wardrobe of women's clothes. While a full tabloid treatment of the story with names and photographs might add to the gaiety of the nation it wouldn't add anything material to appreciation of his more public work.

But then again, on a slightly different tack, it's remarkable how real sexual irregularity leads to financial irregularity. If you are married and you take on a mistress, by some strange alchemy, you will start taking your mistress on business trips with you paid for by the company. You will trade a first-class ticket for two business-class tickets. You will claim for dinners together and weekends away.

Rampant sex can often damage judgment. Is it to do with the hormones released in the process? Damaged judgment is probably a necessary pre-condition for very rampant sex. But there are stories like that of the minister re-allocating public funds on the basis of very special treatment in the bed of Auckland's most talented bisexual woman, and in such stories we see private behaviour spilling over into the public coffers.

On a more basic level, people with conventional morals ask the question: "If he cheats on his wife why wouldn't he cheat on me?"

But the real reason the public is interested in the sex lives of public figures isn't always so high-minded. There is, of course, a mixture of voyeurism, titillation and the ordinary sadism in seeing greatness fall from its pedestal.

In Britain they manage these things so much better. David Mellor, cabinet minister, is found sucking the toes of a courtesan and is fired; the *Sun* runs the headline: *From toe job to no job!*

Sometimes, sex scandals can be a useful index of decadence. After the Tories in England had been in power for a decade their politicians started being found in bed with women. This lapse in traditional Tory values was partly corrected when that promising young MP was found dead on his kitchen table with an orange in his mouth, a noose round his neck, dressed in a rubber suit and a gas mask.

But in this country, male politicians are strangely arousing for a certain sort of woman. It's the Kissinger Principle: "A secretary of state is never too ugly to get a date". The idea of Muldoon being attractive to women might be taking the Kissinger Principle too far (but then you'd think Kissinger would take the Kissinger principle too far). Muldoon was said to be an active off-the-ball player.

In the '70s a notional newspaper called not the *Evening Standard* but the *Double Standard* was invented. It wasn't published, but advertisements for it were. Thus, flysheets were pasted up saying things like *What do Helen, Angela and Mary have in common?* (They were all rumoured to be Muldoon's mistresses.) More straightforwardly, another flyer said, *Rooting pig shot in Ngaio – PM safe.*

For all the revisionism about what a kind man Muldoon was, he would nonetheless be eligible for a charge of sexual assault or even attempted rape. When Zelda Finlay (one of the most attractive political wives of the time, and one who still exudes a personal magic) found herself alone in an office on a parliamentary sofa with Robert Muldoon, he made something more than an affirmative pass at her.

"He lurched forward and grabbed me; suddenly his mouth was on mine – that sloppy kiss I'll remember till I die. I pushed him away, and said: 'Thea's a good friend of mine, and there's Martyn up there in that office.' But he paid no attention and he came back all over me, forcing that necessary part of himself onto me. Oh, and seeing that face, that dreadful face close up *so much more awful when it was close*, I shall remember till I die."

In that vignette of the younger, vigorous Muldoon (and very much better looking than he would become a decade later) is revealed much of the presumptuousness of power, a *droit de seigneur* that prefigured his subsequent psychological decline.

David Lange's affair with his speech writer was a sexual relationship with wider significance. Margaret Pope was providing more comfort, solace and inspiration than his cabinet colleagues. Testimony from the time suggests she was developing into the Yoko Ono of the fourth Labour government, and the two of them retreated into a private world. No-one will ever now know what the net effect of all this was. No-one's that interested anymore.

What this country needs – if for nothing else than to express its unique capacity and talent for gossip – is a *Private Eye*-style publication. Now, it's true the British, being ruder than any other nation, have a natural advantage in excellence in the gutter (and this comes from a long, historic tradition of invective and abuse – "*Hail mitred hog!*" was an early welcome for a Bishop arriving in Oxford) but we come from a British tradition and the lessons they have to teach can be quickly picked up.

Queen Victoria, for instance, achieved deep unpopularity in the early part of her reign. Indeed, a vile satire was published on her wedding day which likened her husband to a railway engine which started out at Virginia Water, passed through Maidenhead, leaving Staines behind (*oh!*). She actually threatened to abdicate unless press criticism levelled off (not a threat you'd risk these days).

Private Eye was the only publication to strike a contrary note when the Emperor Hirohito came to visit Britain. The media went into one of its periodic fits of submission and bent over backwards to exculpate the Emperor from any involvement in the Second World War. The cover of *Private Eye* showed a picture of the frail old man with the caption, *There's a nasty nip in the air! The Eye says: Piss off bandy legs!*

There are a number of other techniques that spin politicians and their Servants may collaborate in.

Prior authority:

"It's not just me that thinks this," is a very important platform.

To get change going you need an independent authority to quote. If you want to change the health system (or the tax system or the superannuation system) you commission the right people to write a report that carries the conclusions you want. Far from being independent bodies charged with elucidating an objective, these bodies are intensely politicised – the more so for their quasi-independent status.

So we all know that a public health plan commissioned by Roger Douglas and written by Alan Gibbs is going to make very different recommendations than a public health plan commissioned by Helen Clark and chaired by Sandra Coney.

During the Aotearoa scandal, Tuku's electorate manager appealed to a far higher authority – the British Conservative party – in his defence of his man. "What's everyone complaining about?" he said, "British MPs do this all the time, they even take money for asking questions in Parliament!" When told by the interviewer that the MPs in question had resigned and would be prosecuted, Tuku's manager laughed and charmingly said, "That's the last time I use *that* example, then."

Spin doctors who think ahead may go so far as to construct lobby groups who can present independent arguments. When advocating a low, flat tax, Act was looking for a body like Americans for Tax Reform (we couldn't find one). These interest groups provide research, polls, quotes, evidence, and pressure to help crystallise and motivate public opinion.

We have bodies like that in New Zealand, from the Business Roundtable to the Coalition for Public Health. They line up roughly like this.

On the right: the Employers and Manufacturers' Federation; the Auckland Chamber of Commerce; any of the economic departments of the trading banks, the Campaign for Better Government, Federated Farmers, the School Trustees Association and so forth.

On the left: the Coalition for Public Health, the Electoral Reform Lobby, the Post-Primary Teachers Association, that lobby group for the unemployed run by Sue Bradford, and goodness knows what else.

All these groups commission surveys, and present evidence that strongly supports the case they are making. Partial as they are, these organisations – having a name, and a staff no matter how small, have far more authority than interested individuals making the same noises.

The right people:

When you have key positions in the establishment filled by certain sorts of people your policy is irresistible.

At a lower level, Bolger's leadership position is better than it looks because much of the party machinery is still loyal to him.

Indeed, past a certain stage it becomes very difficult to get anyone of contrary opinion into organisations you have stocked with your own. For instance, right wingers won't accept a job in the Law Commission. The generally lefty atmosphere means that they will be opposed on principle, they'll achieve nothing, they'll spend two years in a hostile environment being laughed at, criticised and treated with contempt. If they wanted work like that they'd go into politics.

That the legal establishment has drifted to the liberal end of the spectrum is clear when we remember that Martyn Finlay was considered the dangerous lefty of the 1960s. He left a legacy of . . . the Matrimonial Property Act. At the time, this subversive Bill (a plot to undermine the foundations of the family) gave married women automatic entitlement to the matrimonial property. Today you would have to be dangerously to the right to argue against this. So while the economic thinking has moved to the right, social thinking has moved equally to the left (except in the case of the Christian Democrats where they advocate the opposite).

The same sort of dominance is evident in the universities. Jane Kelsey says that the left-wing academics have been silenced by an oppressive conspiracy of new-right ideologues. She speaks from a university department where she has been employed in perpetuity, along with allies in the fight against like Tim Hazledine and Keith Rankin and other teepee-economists.

Stunts:

It's often a shorthand way of communicating a message to devise plans of symbolic value. Punching a photographer or a demonstrator says a great deal about your personal courage, pluck and sense of humour (none of it very good of course, but a certain constituency likes that).

When I was working in Jim Bolger's office, he said he wanted recommendations for projects that would be popular and not cost anything. (This sensible strategy was the same one that gave us the MMP referendum – a popular option that wouldn't cost anything. This is by the way.) The best of the ideas I came up with was to make New Zealand territorial waters a whale sanctuary, to have an international whale conference here every year and commission some electronic musician to compose a whale opera and so forth. I can say this without embarrassment because it happened four years ago. A week is a long time in politics, but four years is unimaginable.

Now, it's still clear that this would have benefits for the country: pictures of New Zealand volunteers pulling stranded whales back into the tide are always hitting the six o'clock news in Berlin and London and Rome. We also had a technical connection with the issue via our New Zealand President of the International Whaling Commission – indeed, it was through our efforts that this body was hijacked and dramatically turned from an industry lobby group into a whale-preservation organisation.

But wait, there's more. The plan would have required no legislation because under the Marine Mammals Act it is already illegal to take whales in our waters. And as a *coup de grace*, the Act was sponsored and shepherded in the late seventies by one Jim Bolger.

Think of the merchandising, the news slots in Berlin, New York, London! Think of the conferences, the boost to the whale-watching industry, the national environmental branding, the tourist draw!

It was impossible for me to get anyone to take the idea seriously. The Minister for the Environment thought about it a moment and said, "It would only be a cosmetic change."

He meant it like it was a bad thing.

When Jim Anderton left Parliament to escape the bruising nature of Parliament (and also the superhuman effort of keeping the five parties of the Alliance together) "to spend more time with his family", it was widely assumed by us chatterers that it was a stunt. Indeed, when Sandra Lee's leadership failed to fire, Jim Anderton's haste to roll her and get back into the fray was given an abrupt lesson by Mat Rata.

The story was that Mat Rata said to him, "If you roll Sandra Lee you'll have such a fight on your hands from me you'll never recover."

Jim asked then what he should do. "Go back to your electorate," he was told, "get your electorate chairman to conduct a poll showing that a large majority want you to come back. Let the media speculate about your return. Let a groundswell build. Give Sandra time to take this information on board, give her space to retire with dignity. And then return as a redeeming hero."

And so it happened, the best-managed stunt in the parliamentary term and a tribute to Mat Rata's skills and his support of Sandra Lee.

The brutal display of professional power:

In America, spin doctors are substantial people in their own right, in effect virtual politicians. And that's starting to happen here. Richard Griffin and Michael Laws, in their different ways and at different times, have had enormous effect on the processes of the state.

Richard Griffin said at the beginning of his press secretary career that it was fascinating going through the looking glass and seeing what was on the other side. Sometimes I say to him that he didn't go through the looking glass until he helped put the Coalition together. It was then that he came off the sidelines and he entered into the political arena, and that he should be careful because he probably hasn't the temperament to be a politician (which, as we know, is a very unusual one).

People of Griffin's capacity can reorganise your mind simply by having the experience, the knowledge, the insight to create space where no space previously existed. Most advisers are less able and some can't be any good at all. When the *Sunday News* rang Deb Morris' office to enquire about the topless picture that was being hawked around by an old flatmate of the minister, the press secretary said: "Is that the photograph you mean, or the video?"

The *video*? Nobody knew there was a *video* in circulation, but thanks to the press secretary every journalist in the country started looking for it.

By contrast, when I Richard Griffin about *Winston First* (an anti-Winston work by Ruth Richardson's ex-press secretary) he was distantly scathing about it. "It misses the point," he said. "It hasn't the measure of the man; it misses his good points." I don't know why I'd assumed the Prime Minister's press secretary would have such a magnanimous attitude to the Prime Minister's nemesis, and the conversation resulted in a couple of paragraphs about Winston's good points the book hadn't recognised, which I thought rather added to the damage.

While Griffin is probably New Zealand's grandest political professional he doesn't wield the power that his counterpart in Britain, Bernard Ingham, was able to for a while.

This was Mrs Thatcher's press secretary in a time of her decadence. It was a last-act scene of executions and persecutions. Ministers were coming and dizzily going and Ingham came to direct the traffic rather than merely report on it. He used to give unattributable briefings to the media, off-the-record conversations in which he would tell the press candidly who was in favour, who was out of favour, who was sliding and who was marked for extinction. To be out of favour, limping, was to be very vulnerable in Mrs Thatcher's Westminster. It took only the smallest indication from Ingham to set the dogs onto the afflicted. In this way, Mrs Thatcher's hands were only ever soiled by choice, in the despatch of her close colleagues.

The *Independent*, the national Fleet Street daily, recognised that such an information bottleneck was a power centre inimical to independent journalism and became the only paper that wouldn't join this lobby system.

Such a press secretary would have found a position under Muldoon; today the Coalition has different dynamics. Both leaders will defend their people as far as they can; they have to keep their end up not just for the public but for their opponents in cabinet.

Ignore the question:

This is such a staple we needn't go into it too far. But if you try to get John Banks actually to deplore the idea of homosexuality he will talk indefinitely about his support for family values. He is too canny to allow anything that sounds like homophobia to find concrete expression.

In the same way, being in an argument with an on-form Winston is like being in a fight in a Glasgow pub. He hits you with everything at once – fists, feet, his head, a chair leg, a broken bottle and the severed arm of your close colleague. He would never admit he was *wrong* – why commit suicide when there is much life and colour ahead?

The release of information – the timing:

When politicians have some lousy news they have to break, 5pm Friday is a good time to release it. It's too late for television, people are less interested in politics over the weekend and by Monday it's already old news (which is no news). And if two jumbos have collided over a volcano, so much the better. Helen Clark had prefigured the sacking of Annette King for some time, but waited until Neil Kirton was fired to actually do the job.

The Serious Fraud Office is no friend of Winston. He repeatedly denounced them in Parliament as being incompetent and corrupt, and he called for the resignation of its director. So when the SFO investigated Tuku's management of the famous television station – and they had plenty of time to decide when to deliver their underwear report – they felt just after the Treasurer's first budget would be an appropriate time.

The Housewife Defence:

"Nothing new here" is a strangely damning thing to say, and it's amazing how it relegates a potentially shocking item of news to banality.

The psychological reality of this is deep. In ordinary life, a housewife scrimps a few dollars out of her budget to pay off a lay-by item in town. When it's hers, she takes it home and is confronted with the problem of how to explain it to her husband. So she hides it about the house and when her husband eventually discovers it she says: "Oh you silly old fool, that's been there for ages, stop complaining!"

Polling:

Language was given to man so that he might conceal his thoughts. Polling was given to politicians to help them conceal theirs.

Polling is why politicians sound so similar at election time. All their research tells them the same things: every focus group produces the same material. People are worried about the social services, they worry New Zealand won't hold, that crime, decaying values and declining standards are endangering the social fabric.

There were a couple of surprises in the research groups I sat in on around the time of the last election. One was the unexpectedly negative view of Jim Bolger. "What would you say to the Prime Minister if he were here?" the researcher asked. "I'd say, *'Shoot those fucking horses!'* one man said, the only swear word in the whole set of six groups. (There'd been that on-again, off-again thing about the Kaimanawa horses). But no-one had a good word to say about him, or anyone else actually, except strangely enough Roger Douglas.

There was one theme underlying nearly everything that was said. It was a theme that no-one would articulate directly. When all groups said they were worried about unemployment, violence in society, increasing crime levels, the development of an underclass, the breakdown of what it meant to be a New Zealander, it came to seem that these were all code words for Maori. This theme, powerful because people suppress it, may become significant for this country.

The anti-Asian sentiments could have been pitched by no-one but Winston; for the time being there is no-one capable of running a One New Zealand campaign to draw on the fear, violence, envy and insecurity of white New Zealanders, but when one emerges we will all be in very serious trouble.

Deny:

Not a shred of evidence!" Winston cried, the day the *Dominion* published the actual travel docket for one of Tuku's more ambitious overseas trips.

Assorted items:

When criticised specifically, issue an action for slander (it costs very little to file the claim), have the matter go sub judice (it will take two years to go to court) and you can refuse to answer any further questions on the matter because it is sub judice. At the last moment, when you have run out of extensions, you can withdraw the suit. Everyone will have forgotten the issue by then anyway.

Leave a confidential leak face down in the photocopier, it looks like a natural mistake. You may have to leave it there more than once – some helpful people return it. Remember: if you find a confidential document in a photocopier, consider who gains most by its publication and who loses. Then imagine what the loser could possibly gain (they are the most likely source).

Never appear alone. A leader alone looks as though they have no followers. Never carry your own bags. If temporarily out of power, arrive in an unmarked taxi (they look like government cars).

8

What can spin doctors do for prominent politicians?

"These disgusting, hard, overcooked croquettes are uneatable."
"Sir, they are biscuits."
"Biscuits? Delicious!"

IN ADVERTISING it is important to tell consumers what it is they are buying. This large, indented glass object for instance – is it an ashtray? Or a paperweight? Or a piece of sculpture? If it isn't labelled, only the price tag will tell me what the creator thinks it is.

And maybe the creators of their products don't know either. When starting a newspaper business in London, I bought thirty thousand old copies of *The Times* from the 1860s. They were to be sold to American tourists as historical records of the American civil war. Four copies were eventually so sold.

However, when they were represented as birthday presents for people to give to their parents and grandparents the business boomed. No-one wanted a historical record of the American civil war; everyone wanted a present with their birthdate printed on it. Same object, new name, different product. This is where advertising reality does have a relationship with political reality.

As we know, in factual matters there is a very wide latitude. For instance, a compulsory superannuation scheme with full equivalent tax cuts. Is this an assault on the freedom of choice New Zealanders enjoy? Or does it increase the freedom for taxpayers to spend their money as they wish? Does it guarantee economic security for the country? Or will it cause a recession by taking money out of circulation? Will it cause house prices to fall as savings are deployed into areas other than housing? Or will it cause house prices to rise as savings funds increase in value?

If you were given an hour's tutorial by Jenny Shipley or Roger Douglas you could be argued into accepting any of these propositions regardless of your political affiliation.

But with people, scope is more limited.

In general terms there's not a great deal consultants can actually do beyond tidying the client up. It's like bringing up children: you may be able to bend their behaviour ten per cent one way or ten per cent the other, the rest is genetically fixed. If you can move a leader through more than this small variation you'll damage the root structure and they won't prosper again.

If the public has taken a strong interest in politicians there may be two or even three ideas attached to them:

Jim Bolger: big-foot, provincial, expedient
Helen Clark: cool, intelligent
Roger Douglas: other-worldly, integrity
Winston Peters: paranoid, thrilling

Richard Prebble: tough, humorous

Jim Anderton: caring

Jenny Shipley: sensible

The reputation thing is also true for governments. The Nats have increased public spending over the last eighteen months by billions, the surpluses are almost gone but they will never be known as anything other than skinflints.

Insofar as other politicians are noticed their media profile is like this:

Bill Birch: fixer (This is changing: he is now quietly cultivating a reputation for boring reliability).

Paul East: dandy

Doug Graham: toff

Simon Upton: ponce

Phil Goff: professional

An interesting side-effect of political reputations is that scandals will only attach themselves to people where they fit the character. When Robyn McDonald spent $35,000 on a trip to Paris in the early days of the Coalition, it took off as a story because the media had Robyn pegged as a shopper. Jonathan Hunt's taxi bill took because he was pegged as having a capacity for self-indulgence. But Helen Clark's $60,000 limousine bill doesn't take at all, it doesn't fit with her profile.

But how tenacious reputations are. Derek Quigley made a speech to the Young Nats at the beginning of the '80s and ever after has been known as the man who stood up to Muldoon.

These reputations, while positive (to be known you usually have to be known for something) are confining.

Certain people can only say certain things. Richard Prebble can't get attention when he talks about education. Helen Clark can't pitch the communal warmth of cigarette factory socialism;

Jim Bolger couldn't sell a recovery to a hostile media even though the stockmarket was doubling, Roger Douglas couldn't pitch a new party to the public even though it had the tightest and most coherent policy base of any.

While we're on that subject, what advice would you as a spin doctor give to Roger Douglas? Advisers are always saying to him: "Keep it simple, don't talk numbers, leave out the compound interest, talk values, give us passion."

As a matter of record that's exactly what he was doing all last year, valiantly and impressively. But it didn't take. It didn't work. People heard what they thought he was saying but it was conditioned by what they thought of Roger. So he gives the "snakes and ladders" speech (all values) but it doesn't make any difference at all in the public perception of him. People in his admiring audience think: "What he says is correct and believable, but I bet there aren't many people who agree with us." There is no solution to this. If there were, Roger would still be Minister of Finance, if not Prime Minister.

In the same way, if you wanted Philip Burdon for prime minister you'd have to face the fact that you can't make a sow's ear out of a silk purse. And you can give Jim Bolger rhetoric, but he won't deliver it. Politicians do what they do, and their consultants can only vary their presentation by that ten degrees each way.

Winston's image of Treasurer has improved the full twenty degrees over the last six months. His new press secretary was talking (remarkably frankly, considering it was on national radio), telling us what he would try and do for his new boss. "I'd want to show him doing solid work on the Budget so he looks the part of the Treasurer. And when I talked to business leaders I'd want to demonstrate I was on top of the economics." By and large, that's worked; nor was the strategy damaged by being announced in public. As Mike Moore says, "Plot in public. It's more discreet."

It conforms to the pattern, because studies show that when people present themselves, their message is received in a variety of ways, but principally by what they are saying, how they are saying it, and how they look (including their body language). One of these impressions is by far the strongest followed closely by another; the least important aspect, obviously when you think about it, is what they say. That may be because they aren't saying anything people want to hear, but that's only part of the story.

The partnership that really worked most effectively was that between Michael Laws and Winston, and between Michael Laws and Neil Kirton. It is worth saying that in spite of not being quite sure of what Michael Laws does, we all agree he is remarkably good at it.

He has a touch that we, his pale imitators, cannot match. Our counterpunches lacked charm, the right weighting, the touch. When he was high in the demonology of Bolger's opponents there was a speech I made at a charity debate in Hastings. There were some very funny lines, I have to say, including: "Michael Laws is a man so completely false that even his hair, which looks like a wig, isn't. There was a rather plangent line: "When we look into the hall of mirrors which constitutes the soul of Michael Laws we see only the distorted reflection of our own lower appetites." And there was a line which made the whole assembly wince and swing decisively to Michael's side (no mean feat in front of a farming audience). It went: "To the questions should drunken child abusers be a) tortured to death or b) given tax incentives Michael Laws will reply: *that depends entirely on how many drunken child abusers there are in my electorate who will vote for me.*" Here was another frontal assault, heavily overweighted, actually embarrassing, and having the opposite effect from what was intended.

Touch is something we just didn't have. When the government was complaining about Paul Holmes' unrelenting criticism during the first Bolger term, you went to the transcripts to substantiate your complaint and were bewildered by the neutral – even positive – messages. The point is, if you've broadcast the words, "The government says economic growth will achieve five per cent next year" you don't have to add, "and I'm the Duchess of York," if you've used a tone of incredulous scorn. Holmes' touch is invariably accurate: he can place the ball in whatever part of the court he chooses it to go.

But Laws is the master of his own environment, and it's a privilege to witness him operating. Everyone was able to admire his 'Chequers' speech of resignation on television, and how he turned a damaging scandal to his credit by presenting himself as a martyr to his own sense of honour.

But it's there in everything he does. Everything he does he does well. I said to him on the phone recently, "While we're on different sides of the paddock I yield to no-one in my admiration of your technical skills."

He replied, "I don't think we *are* on different side of the paddock. We both believe people ought to be able to choose. I am a socialist, but I'm a democrat before I'm a socialist." Isn't that brilliant?

His touch is wonderfully apparent when you listen to the phone message on his call minder. He begins his domestic message with his wife's name then his. His voice proceeds with a faint hesitation a shyness almost, almost as if you had disturbed him at prayer, roused him from a deep meditation, and this invites the caller into an intimacy where humility and respect struggle for the upper hand. You know you will be listened to by this man, you will be recognised and respected; you are invited into his sanctum where the simple act, say, of taking tea with each other will be invested with a significance that is personal, gentle and meaningful. And that's just his phone message.

He has discerned the rules of engagement in the media and is able to calculate the weight of his punches perfectly. He interrupts Paul Holmes by talking under him, not over.

He has understood as most of us have not that an over-weighted punch will cause you to lose your balance. So, Ian Fraser might assume Bolger is unpopular enough to give a laborious and unforgiving going-over but the viewers are just as likely to feel aggrieved for the victim. Why? They see him in a fight like they have at home, being unfairly accused, or abused, or not listened to.

Muriel Newman publishes another of her *Live on an Oily Rag* books and is invited onto television where she is done like a dinner by Susan Wood and Pam Corkery. But the overkill produces sympathy for Muriel on the talkbacks the following day.

On a wider canvas, seatbelt ads showing a body firing through a windscreen and landing on someone else's bonnet actually make me laugh out loud. And as for that poor blighter doing 124 kilometres an hour who gets hit by a car on the wrong side of the road and then gets properly slagged by his wife – we all say: "*Get a divorce!*"

When we started Act, the management was constantly looking for "hot buttons" to push and were confused and disappointed when the buttons were pushed and nothing happened. Act was talking social crisis, declining educational standards, lower tax levels – all of which concern a middle-class audience. The buttons failed to fire and it bewildered everyone involved. "What do you have to *do*? we asked rhetorically, daily. The hot button that year was actually Asian immigration. Winston raised it – and it took him Lazarus-like from the margin of error back into contention for prime minister.

The crucial point was that it was Winston's issue. No-one else had the credentials to run that line. The subtext was thrilling with Winston's paranoia and conspiracy and dislike of Asians for their money and their numbers and the way they drive. Winston the avenger for the dispossessed, the one who warns of threats, who drags conspiracies into the open. If anyone else had identified Asian immigration as an issue and tried to run it (assuming they'd had the brass neck to do so) it probably would have failed to fire.

Admittedly this was Terry Heffernan's (the old Social Credit candidate) work rather than Michael's but the point holds, I feel.

Michael's good at all this because he's done it himself. Usually the gulf between communication professionals and politicians is enormous. Commentators live in the luxury of retrospect; advisers live in the luxury of anonymity – the only can they carry is their job. Michael Wall put his finger on the difference when writing a speech for Jim Bolger: "I'm in favour of the Prime Minister leading with his chin. I'm more in favour of it than he is, but then it's his chin, not mine."

Politicians are different in kind. And this is never more obvious than at the cross-over point when a professional critic or spin doctor attempts the transition. Funnily enough, Pam Corkery though she talks like a tannoy and has that *mouth*, has probably made one of the more successful transitions. Denis Welch is a more characteristic example. He used to do so well writing his insightful and amusing political commentaries – but as a politician he was a nitwit. His career came to end on camera – he was asked during the Wellington Central campaign (which there was a chance of winning, it seemed to us) what he would do if his child wouldn't fasten their seatbelt. He replied the family would get out of the car and not go on the trip. The reaction against draconian unilateral government action was at its height at that time but the media couldn't swallow that.

The plain fact is that commentators and communicators should know their place. A quote from McAlpine again:

> The Servant will understand the grandeur of his role, for in the heart of every Servant there lies a Prince – a desire to be noble and brave and successful. It is proper that this should be so, for the Prince is a symbol of these things. But, Servant, let that inner Prince lie still, for ambition is easily spotted and becomes the wasting disease of the Servant. Contain this force, this ambition and use its energy only in the service of your master, and in time you may become a Prince among Servants.

Anyone who's had anything to do with a prime minister feels proud of it. So we like to use the unnatural mode of address "Prime Minister". These words make us feel important. It doesn't sound a very New Zealand trait but using the words Prime *Minister* provides a strange and rather twisted thrill of submission. (As an uncomfortable aside, I take this attitude further than most. I don't even like people saying Maggie Thatcher, I find it too personal. I always call her Mrs Thatcher, even while I'm rocking with laughter in front of her TV performance.)

That British background can be disabling; it is different in America. Robert Kennedy was praised for his lack of familiarity with his brother the President. In public Robert always called

JFK Mr President, even while other, lesser associates were using his Christian name.

Of course, every time Robert Kennedy said Mr President he was also saying to all the consultants, speech writers, ministers, hot-shots, Camelot courtiers and freeloaders in the room: "Hey, schmoozers, this man is a *President*! I'm his *brother* and even I call him Mr *President!* Let's have some *respect* round here!" (a subtle way of imposing his status on the room).

But working for the Prime Minister in his office (as opposed to his department) has a political thrill because when he goes, you go. The pharaoh dies and you all troop into the tomb with him. The tomb in those days seemed an imminent proposition to nearly everyone except Bolger himself (see Tenth Law). I had lunch with a government whip at the time who said: "Everyone in the backbench knows there is no possibility of Jim's leading us into the next election. The whole backbench knows that."

In this context, spin was no effectual use for Jim Bolger, nothing could get traction. The best thing Michael Wall did for him in those days was to cancel the Monday morning press conferences where the toreadors would dance around the pawing bull plunging one dart after another into his neck.

Jim Bolger was the first prime minister in living memory to reach such low levels of public approval. We remember how he swept into power promising a new start, to abolish the surcharge and to found a new society, "the decent society". For reasons that most of us have now forgotten (the BNZ, the $5 billion deficit predicted by Treasury), his first actions included slashing benefits and increasing the surcharge. The public, after six years of hidden agendas and political turmoil, turned on him. And the media did too. "Negative" is the wrong word. They were rabid. Nothing he could do or say would be reported neutrally. He couldn't even say that there were proportionately more Maori in prison than Pakeha without the media calling him a liar. It was the era of gaffes.

There was a Sunday meeting in which we were considering the forthcoming by-election in Tamaki, and how the government was so far down in the polls that keeping the seat looked dicey, and the fact that Sir Robert Muldoon seemed to prefer the Tamaki seat go to Labour rather than to his erstwhile colleagues (see Second Law of Darkness: *friends are more dangerous than enemies*). Indeed, he had already expressed a preference in the House by criticising David Kirk's standing for selection by saying, "We've got too many backs in Parliament; we need more forwards."

Anyway, in this troubled situation, Michael began a rhetorical trope for Bolger which had the hairs standing up on the back of my neck, as A.E. Housman said poetry is supposed to do: "If losing Tamaki is the price we have to pay for the lowest inflation in the western world, we will pay that price. If Tamaki is the price for the fastest rate of employment growth in the world we will pay that price. If Tamaki is the price for" (I forget what just at the moment) "we will pay that price *because we will never go back to the failed policies of the past!*"

The Prime Minister went into the press conference the following day and caused enormous gratitude in the media corps by saying: "It's possible we may lose Tamaki."

Subeditors fell on this. Headlines gleefully him denounced as a gaffe-maker extraordinary, commentators reviled him for striking a fatal blow at party confidence, the political scientist with the cat-like toupee sadly said on *Holmes* how unprecedented it was.

It's true that Bolger's statement had less brio than Michael's. He had taken out the rhetoric. When you translate poetry into another language only the prose gets through, the poetry is left behind. But when you took out the rhetoric you were left with a gaffe.

But as a postscript, it must be said that in the peculiar way Bolger had, he said something which was widely derided and it turned out to be both useful and true. In Tamaki, the party organisation which had been riven by dissent was galvanised into action and returned Clem Simich quite comfortably (he was the one sent to Wellington with "a message"; no-one ever found out what it was).

The connection that people can make with audiences is the first talent of politicians. As Jim Bolger's speech writer I always advised him to deliver impromptu speeches. He came across better when speaking off the cuff (or from the heart as it might be said) and he could connect in a way that the typed speech notes interrupted. As I was being paid per speech this advice was disinterested; when I went onto salary I intensified my efforts in this direction but with no greater success.

In those days, as a speech writer, I was in the category of "intelligent subordinate" which, in McAlpine's terms, is only just less trouble than he's worth. The most obviously unsuitable speech I wrote for him was to be delivered in front of Queen Juliana of the Netherlands on her state visit and consisted of a blistering condemnation of restrictive trading practices in the European Union, and it advised her that the walls they were building round their trading bloc "don't just keep us out, *they keep you in*". This isn't how prime ministers talk to visiting queens, incidentally.

I plead inexperience, it all happened two or three lifetimes ago when I was barely forty. On a more reasonable level I introduced "virtuous circle" into the conventional wisdom, but my plan for the Meat Board to buy a million acres of Russia, and export two thousand farm workers to grow lamb and feed Moscow was less successful.

But as we know, Bolger is marvellously loyal and put up with me for over two years, but I never really got the hang of writing what he wanted written.

I gave him a speech which labelled the three Acts – Employment Contracts Act, the Reserve Bank Act and the Fiscal Responsibility Act "the founding documents of the recovery". Bolger crossed out the "founding documents of the recovery" and substituted "the three very important pieces of legislation without which the recovery wouldn't have happened".

Such is Bolger, and such he still is. He is not comfortable with these posh, rhetorical flourishes. He will allow his hair and his suits, and that smile someone must have taught him, but he remains stubbornly true to his own instincts (that's why he's stayed where he is). Maybe he subscribes to Dr Johnson's advice to find the phrase in the text you've written of which you are most proud and strike it out.

But a Servant would be able to write speeches for Bolger that expressed his nature. But the speech he needed to deliver I couldn't have persuaded him to deliver. It would have been a speech without notes on the subject of education.

He would start on a conventional line about how important education is for children, the most important thing they can be given. Then he would move into a personal story of his boyhood and how he ran the family farm while his father was away at war, and how he had to quit school so early as a result. But then he'd point out to all the children who weren't doing well at school today that school isn't everything. People who fail at school can still find work, can love their families and their children, and if they work hard and do well in the world . . . they might even become Prime Minister, it's happened before.

It is the stuff of late night conversations and would work for Bolger in a way that it wouldn't for Winston – or indeed, anyone. You wouldn't want to hear this sort of thing from Mike Moore, if it applied to him, or from Helen Clark because their dynamics are different.

Bolger has a remoteness from the public (and they resent it). He has to reinvent himself now in the end-game of his career – because a perfectly good school of thought says he can still win his leadership battle, and maybe even win easily.

And leaders are so difficult to manage, it's not surprising they aren't managed very much. For instance, I doubt whether there is any substantial political figure who could master the basic skill of, say, knowing when to stop (after you've started, everyone's longing for you to stop).

I was listening to Jim Bolger answering a question about Winston's Winebox appeal and the answer included an assessment of the New Zealand economy from a visiting English expert, a measure of local business confidence, the value of the dollar, the pain of kiwifruit growers, and the fact that Indian exporters (like our own) have the highest level of five-year optimism in the region.

An otherwise inconspicuous British backbencher called Nick Budgen made a media profile by doing something very odd: he answered television reporters' questions very clearly, and when he'd answered what he'd been asked he abruptly stopped speaking. The first time he did this, in a live outside broadcast from the Palace of Westminster during the period of the coup that rolled Mrs Thatcher, the reporter was caught unawares. He left the sort of inviting pause which politicians have traditionally filled with a subsidiary point. You could feel the off-camera reporter making rolling "what else?" gestures with his hand but Budgen just glared. Eventually another question was fumblingly produced (that was answered in two words, discomforting the interviewer even further).

To master this skill requires a whole different mindset, a new emotional apparatus, a sense of confidence that the silence you leave when you finish will be eloquent. This can't really be taught except by experience. You need so much presence of mind to be able to summon the shortest thing of interest to say.

In New Zealand, one politician has mastered the opposite talent – the rolling flow of subsidiary points: Jim Anderton. It is marvellous how much he can put into one masterful answer. It's not that he never stops – he can pause in the middle of an answer, even to search for a word – but he does something very different when he moves to another point. He moves to the new point without any discernible pause whatsoever. An interviewer couldn't put a scalpel between the end of one point and the beginning of another.

To realise the technological point of Jim's skill here, you might remember that there used to be a momentary pause between programmes and commercials on television until it was realised that videos could be instructed to record a programme but stop when the commercials came on and start again when the commercials had finished – now they're seamless.

If you're a person this isn't easy to do. You need to be relaxed; you need to be totally in command of your last sentence and casting forward the first sentence of a wholly new point. It's actually extremely difficult and who knows how long Jim has been working on it. But the value for money is marvellous – you ask him one question and get three answers.

On the wider scale, knowing when to stop might apply to knowing when to leave office. There have been many elections where a government reasonably expected to lose but scrambled a win (often with the help of a new face as leader) – but in the subsequent election the party is comprehensively hammered. They are beaten so badly that it might have been preferable to have lost the previous one. In 1925, a New Zealand war hero became leader and was done like a dinner the next time out.

In 1969, the new face of Muldoon as finance minister gave Holyoake a narrow win – they were landslid out in the '72 election. Muldoon himself slipped in against the odds in 1981 and let Labour start its revolutionary changes the following time. George Bush, Paul Keating and John Major all won an election too many this decade. Maybe history will show that Bolger himself went a bridge too far in his pact with New Zealand First.

But to go willingly into opposition and into a leadership contest is to go willingly into that dark courtyard with the gallows and the block. Why would you do it? (That of course is why America has term limits.)

But there are things image people can and do tell politicians, and they are instructions that can be carried out because politicians would rather do them than not do them. Roosevelt said he was always obeyed by his children. "I take care to find out what it is they want to do and advise them strongly to do it," he said.

But finally, spin doctors and servants and Servants have a limited role because the truth will emerge. Character will out. Voters aren't stupid. No matter how often stupid people say voters aren't stupid, the fact is, voters aren't stupid.

Actually voters are stupid in the sense that they exist in a political stupor, but their assessments of politicians are accurate, in the same way that children assess their teachers accurately. The media has an intimate role in the process of revelation and assessment – and not always the one they think.

9

Two tribes

THE political world broadly splits into two: there is a psychological apparatus that links all the attitudes of each of the two tribes of left and right. This left wing/right wing terminology is currently out of fashion. Commentators like to say the terms are less relevant. And sometimes you see an example of that. Act is a party with left-wing objectives (universal access to social services) with right-wing delivery mechanisms (companies competing to sell us health and savings policies) and this is a source of confusion to the electorate.

Nonetheless, there is the great ideological battle which is still being fought and it is fought around one defining principle, between those who believe that more vigorous state action will help build communities and those who believe less state action will create greater prosperity and happiness. That divide is still meaningful and still connects with a range of seemingly unrelated issues.

Broadly speaking, then, people who don't believe in examinations for school children also tend to believe that global warming is a threat to be addressed with environmental legislation. It's interesting to ask the question, why do those who believe trades unions have a benign effect on society also believe in higher state spending (except for defence) and also believe in more lenient sentences for drug users and affirmative action for minorities. Why is it that those who don't believe in social Darwinism also don't approve of genetic engineering? These are, in general, left-wing attitudes and most proceed directly from a suspicion of and hostility to the demands of capitalism.

Conversely, why do people who believe in lower state spending (except for defence) also believe in stronger laws against drug takers? Why are those people who want stricter examination standards in schools also the ones who would have been in favour of the Springboks '81 tour? This tribe believes a Ministry of Children to be a silly idea but generally favours the idea that private school fees should be tax deductible, that examinations should be winched up in school and that spelling is more important than self-expression for eight-year-olds. These are generally associated with right-wing attitudes and are all sympathetic to the demands of capitalism.

For the indolent this theory has some predictive power, and I'm afraid to say I use it myself. For instance, there's a scheme being floated by the Ministry of Education. Children can choose whether they're assessed internally or by exams. I don't know what I think about this until an education officer says on the news: "This sets up an A and B stream where, in the public mind, the examination stream is considered superior. I think students should have a choice but it's regrettable this notion of superiority is part of it."

And because I know on what side of the argument the Department of Education normally is, and what side of the argument I'm generally on, now I know what to think. It's deplorable, of course, it's lazy, but it's universal, even under the new consensuality of MMP. Parliament has just gone through two debates for identical Bills: to make membership of student unions voluntary. One is being proposed by Act, the other by National. The former is voted down decisively, the latter is sent up for further discussion. "We would never support an Act proposal," a Coalition MP is quoted as saying.

It makes things a lot simpler at any rate, as long as the parties stick to their principles (assuming they have any to begin with).

But then, conversely, New Zealand First has been proposing Act New Zealand's superannuation plan almost verbatim and Act hasn't wanted to support it partly on philosophical grounds (the compulsion is out of synch with the general liberty-thrust of the party) but also because it puts Act on the wrong side of the paddock.

These psychological divisions may go back to the actual beginning of mankind. An anthropologist writing in the *Guardian* described Neanderthal man (short, dark, communal-minded) and how, twenty thousand years ago, he was almost obliterated by Cro-Magnon man. Cro-Magnons (tall, sun-worshipping individualists) find their most potent modern expression in Mrs Thatcher; Neanderthals, the article said, find their modern expression in the Welsh.

So these two tribes still exist, still have vigorous identities – individualists versus communitarians, owners versus workers, personal achievers versus carers-and-sharers – historically, almost genetically at odds with each other (the first act of human history after all was genocide).

There is a deep security in this left-wing, communal view of the world. We all know this feeling from having been part of a social unit, a squad, a team, a cast, a gang when we were young. In adolescence as in socialism, friendship is more important than money – so the group, the team, the gang will always have random elements in it, some very unsuitable, losers, maybe. But you don't eject them; you are loyal to each other because you are all part of each other's destiny. You look after each other whether it's in your immediate interests or not; you'll stick by each other whether the police are coming, or the other side's got a knife. The random element in our cast of friends is good for personal growth; evolutionary theory tells us this.

But, principally, that group feeling is very sweet. When you are in the cast of a play a sense of intimacy gathers around you, both physical and social. When you fit into a school or a team you develop a profound security knowing that you have people on your left and right who will support you. The belief that you can rely on your neighbour when times are hard is a source of warmth.

And as for people, so for countries. New Zealand is just emerging from a boisterous adolescence into a young maturity. New Zealand used to be famous for that lend-us-your-lawnmower socialism. But it may have been more an expression of national character than a political doctrine.

Perhaps it wasn't until the English trades unionists came over and were accorded the respect that international experts have always enjoyed here, and with their class antagonisms and sophisticated techniques they politicised that inchoate feeling, these two ways of being that contend with each other.

The view from the right – the less-government, lower-tax perspective – has less feeling in it. It is, however, in the current millennial environment, unanswerably more effective. People on the right say politics is a filthy business in many ways and they doubt that it's a job that actually has to be done.

People on the left say the forces that are running through the world are so frightening and impersonal we need the protection of the state to raise our families.

There is a great deal to be said on either side of this argument.

In America a pedestrian trips on a paving stone and sues their local authority. While we scoff, politicians have to balance the indolence and incompetence of local bodies with the citizens' need to look where they are putting their feet. In the middle, the media can vigorously blame and console both sides.

But separate from this daily debate something much larger is happening in the world. The nibbling away of the state is a worldwide trend which expresses the vitality of capitalism, and the continuity of an economic history that started with the rise of the merchant classes in the middle ages.

Personally, I believe the force of history will drive politics willy-nilly towards the smaller state and lower-tax model. In the absence of an excoriating war (the Middle East goes up, perhaps, or the Gulf of Tonkin), we are in for an extended period of non-inflationary growth as markets and manufacturers open up in China and India. Enormous advances will be made in technology, computers with artificial intelligence, nanotechnology, genetic engineering, the application of theoretical physics.

Governments can neither compete nor control these forces, they can only ride them. Politicians know this, deep down, they know their carnival is over. The function of politicians is now to manage the process of orderly political withdrawal from the economy.

Watching the state pull out from areas of national life has a familiar look to it. It's like watching the break-up of the British Empire, the withdrawal of British power from colonies and territories and dependencies all over the world where they had administered their well-meaning but often alien justice among people who rarely expressed much gratitude. Among the Brits Go Home! and the riots and the passive demonstrations, the imperial will to power was worn down, and for better and for worse, they went home.

In the same way, the politicians' empire is increasingly dismantled at home. The tide is going out. Their influence is fading. They are packing their tents, taking ceremonial farewells and handing power over to the natives. The occupied territories – ports, airlines, airports, railways, telecommunications, banking, service industries, insurance companies, dairy farms, schools even – are granted more self-determination.

To some colonies freedom brought terror and death, to others it brought prosperity and confidence. It's probably important that we prepare to be on the positive side of that particular ledger.

These world views find media expression in a typically covert way in New Zealand. In Britain it's the overt opposite: newspaper information is so intensely politicised that you don't know what you are reading unless you know who's publishing it. Newspapers select their news stories to illustrate and support the paper's entrenched position. Indeed, the same news story with the same wording will have a totally different effect in the *Telegraph* than in the *Guardian.* Imagine a report of a social worker working on repressed memory syndrome who has been beaten up by policemen. In one paper readers will think "Scandalous!" In the other, readers will think, "Good job!"

Because the daily papers here don't compete directly with each other (they are all prisoners of their classifieds), their politics change according to the spirit of the times or the mood of the moment. The *Herald* has moved from a sort of Alliance sympathy to a brisker pragmatism, especially in the leader and op-ed pages. The *Dominion* similarly moved to the right in the same pages, but neither editor seems to have convincing influence over the spin of the news stories.

There is much to be said on both sides of that question, too.

But the most important filter that is applied to information obtains in television. It is the most important because it is structural, it's how the system works. What gets into the news depends on what television editors want, but what they want isn't immediately apparent.

This is a secret I was made privy to during a serious lunch engagement. We were five bottles into the eight, and at about the time honest working people were home sitting down to their tea, my friend gave me the secret in a simple, almost inconspicuous statement.

"We never do stories about issues," he explained. "We only do stories about people."

Suddenly a whole set of tumblers fell into place. A couple of years previously, Act had been trying to get compulsory superannuation on the media agenda. It was an impossible task; none of us knew why we couldn't get the largest economic fact of New Zealand life onto the news agenda. There wasn't anyone to pitch it. We had Roger Douglas, an other-worldly creature floating above his chair and talking about the power of compound interest but that didn't count as a people story.

New politicians go to Parliament determined to do something about poverty, or state monopolies or the health system, but they find the media are uninterested in their views unless they can produce a relevant human drama set in the area of concern.

Superannuation got on the media agenda only when Winston took an interest in it and got a referendum going. The issue had become connected to people. The media sensed that if the scheme failed at the referendum:

1) Winston's credibility would be severely damaged. This would punish him for having gone with National instead of Labour, and

2) Jenny Shipley's campaign to be leader would have a better chance of unseating Jim Bolger.

So, whatever the pros and cons of the superannuation argument (and you'd think if two characters like Douglas and Peters agree on something there must be something going for it), the people outcomes were far more compelling.

In the same way, they say that visuality and symbol have taken over from analysis. Winston was furious when TV3 broadcast him tripping over a lighting cable on his way to the podium, and then ignored the speech. But if Nick Smith were to trip on a television cable before making a speech you wouldn't broadcast that (why would you want to?) When Winston does the same thing it's irresistible (why would you try to resist?)

Was there more interest in Tuku's underpants than in the future of Maori broadcasting? Almost certainly there was – and that's because Tuku's underpants are attached to a person, and Maori broadcasting is an issue.

In general terms, news stories need a victim. That's the first thing. You need a victim you can sympathise with, and then you need a villain to blame. And as for the hero – you have the reporter jostling with the politician (the champion) for halo-rights.

This is a strategy that applies mainly to television in this country – in Britain the tabloid papers follow the same sort of rule. In the flickering, erotic fairy tale of tabloid journalism you have monsters, dragons, maidens, witches, and the forces of truth, fairness and justice battle with the forces of the dark.

The flickering, erotic fairytale signifies a very large strategy that underlies the dumbing-down of television. The right hate this more than the left, not so much because they generally agitate for higher standards in all areas, but because left-wing politics favour the victim-villain theory of communication.

But despite the increasingly sketchy audiences and increasingly sophisticated viewers, the fact remains – if it hasn't happened on television it hasn't happened.

10

The Laws of Darkness

1 *Always accuse your enemies of your own most obvious faults.*

• Muldoon accused the Labour Party of being socialists.

• Michael Laws accused National backbenchers of disloyalty.

• Jim Anderton accused Peter Shirtcliffe of trying to sabotage the economy.

• Winston accuses everyone of making baseless, scurrilous, scumbag accusations.

• Helen Clark accuses Roger Douglas of playing personality politics.

• Jim Anderton accuses John Delamere of trying to get Alamein Kopu out of the Alliance.

• Jane Kelsey accuses the right of being caught in a time-warp.

This law started life as a theory first observed in marriage. The data for it consisted of arguments that sounded like:

"You're lazy!"

"But that's what *you're* like!"

"Oh you're pathetic, that's all you can say, *that's what you're like, that's what you're like!*"

This law draws its power from therapeutic theory on the one hand (projection) and international rugby on the other (get your retaliation in first).

It may be that this law can predict as well as assert. There was a time when Winston's favoured term of abuse was "fascist!" The *Shipley's List* billboard authorised by Winston before the last election caused a row, and rightfully so. It was a reference to the Holocaust film *Schindler's List* and showed a queue of dispirited citizens in an interminable queue for a hole in the wall waiting for treatment or (the hidden implication) extermination. (Fear of extermination is a real fear among the sort of people who support politicians like Winston. In America, the neutron bomb was characterised as a bomb that would kill only black people.)

There are politicians who can have tendencies towards fascism as it is a philosophy of power that relies on paranoia and charisma – this was Muldoon's most obvious weakness, and his slide into national socialism was pronounced. However, there is a control mechanism in the New Zealand psyche. Although quite a large constituency likes the tough-guy posture that fascism requires, and although there is a mob mentality very much in evidence, there is also a strong anti-militaristic theme running through New Zealand, a reluctance to accept the uniform-wearing that seems also to be an integral part of the show, and a liberal revulsion against the genre.

But fear of fascism should be kept in the back of the mind, because it is remarkable how quickly the tenor of an organisation, even a government, can change; and perhaps it requires paranoids – who are more sensitive than healthy observers – to monitor the increase in swagger and knuckle and muscle in the corridors of power. To that extent the politically correct cowering and the consensualising have an upside.

2 *Beware friends, they're more dangerous than enemies.* When this is said to serious politicians they instinctively agree, whether they can think of any examples or not. It hits them on a visceral level.

"My opponents are in front of me, my enemies are behind me." Maurice Williamson is understandably fond of quoting Gladstone who uttered this in the House of Commons (as in the House of Representatives, you speak facing your opponents with your back to your own party).

Jenny Bloxham, sometime vice-president of New Zealand First, would understand this: when the stamp warrant scandal broke (she used eighty dollars of her parliamentary postage allowance to register her private car), the unofficial message from the party hierarchy to the media was: "Hang her out to dry."

A large front-page story in the *Herald* gave Tau Henare an unusually good write-up. "Henare blasts Australians as mongrels" the headline ran (two days before the Bledisloe, it strikes a chord) and he said he was disgusted by the way the Australians had described his close colleague Winston Peters. It wasn't quite what Winston wanted however, as he was over in Canberra meeting the very people his deputy was abusing.

To plant a poisonous thought in someone's mind about your enemy – praise your enemy. The poisonous burr will go in unsuspected; the praise evaporates quickly, the burr endures.

People being what they are, they like to disagree, to prove

you wrong, you point out things you hadn't considered. Therefore, if you are enraged by your colleagues' failure to get a story up and running in the media, you say: "I think Ken was right to save his contacts in the media for a bigger story." Your colleagues will naturally take a robustly different view.

In the same way, to stimulate greater revelations from a gossip, mildly defend the person they're attacking; a) it makes you look good, and b) provokes them to produce the deep stuff.

A television interviewer used this law cleverly the day after the Winebox judgment had been issued. He got Charles Sturt on air and asked him: "You've had time to sleep on this. Are you softening towards Winston Peters?" You can imagine the response. But a pro-Winston question would have sounded like: "Charles Sturt: Do you hate Winston Peters for having destroyed your career and your credibility?" Sturt's first words would have to have been, "I *don't* hate him," followed shortly by "my career isn't destroyed," and finishing up with, "my credibility is perfectly all right, thank you very much."

Those who seek to persuade will find it more difficult if they relentlessly attack. You must alternate violence with affection and friendliness. The dynamics of an abusive marriage are worth studying for aspiring politicians.

The converse of this law suggests that enemies are more valuable than friends, and there is evidence that this is also true.

Enemies define you more accurately and effectively than friends. When you attack bodies or individuals people will respond to you far more vividly than if you are praising your allies. "I want more enemies," was a principle successfully deployed by the late Sir Robert Muldoon.

When they are starting up, parties are required to punch

above their weight because everyone else is bigger. In Act's early days hardly anyone could be persuaded to take a swing back (they knew their prestige would go down and Act's would go up). But John Banks obliged because he can't help himself, and Winston was kind enough to walk off a stage rather than share it with Rodney Hide and be photographed by the *Herald* in the process (people story, people story!) but by and large politicians rather exclusively recognise their own level and stick to it.

3 *Hatred can be disarmed by trivial acts of courtesy.*
When Bolger and Peters got together over the Coalition, one school of thought saw it as a fatal embrace. They said that it was the final act in the tragedy, the final conflict in their battle would be fought out, the hatred was so deep, so intense, so embedded in history they couldn't both survive. Two go into the Coalition, one comes out.

In the event, they got on extraordinarily well. Reports came back about their sitting up late into the night talking about their fathers. The reason? Prodigal Winston had returned to a welcome of respect by his peers. His anger evaporated, his charm returned.

The appearance of hatred may occasionally be enlivened by genuine anger – but it's rare for people to hate anyone (unless of course they're married to them).

The converse of this is also true. Trivial acts of discourtesy can sometimes be the final straw. Mat Rata left the Labour Party because there was a crush on the parliamentary bench and the occupants wouldn't make room for him. He left the chamber, and the party.

Jim Anderton is said to have abandoned Parliament actually because a staffer had made an appointment for him in a remote meeting hall and given him the wrong date. "It's *next* week.

Lucky it wasn't last week, or you would have missed it altogether," she is reported to have said. That was it for Jim; the bruising brutality of Parliament was one thing, but this was *it*.

The standard of typing can do it for anyone. In one of our perennial office battles Rodney Hide was decisively outmanoeuvred by the management. The standard of typing in the office wasn't high, and if you were wanting to get a dozen letters out a day it could take two or three days to get them all completed. As Rodney's exasperation increased it was put about that Rodney (brilliant, but mercurial) needed a holiday. It became impossible for him to send back a letter five times for its typing errors in anything other than a monotone otherwise the staff would report it around, "The strain's telling on Rodney again; he really should take that holiday."

4 *In the moment of victory you are at your weakest.*

There was a moment when we had inflicted a fatal wound, as we thought, on one of our enemies in the party. His credibility among the senior hierarchy was shattered; he had admitted defeat. Six weeks later he was still there. Yes, we had prevailed, we had taken Berlin: this was the time to press on to Moscow. Had Churchill's advice been followed there may have been no cold war, no evil empire.

But victory is exhausting. When you've won you're weakest. Like the All Blacks forty points ahead it's easy to believe you've won – but when you hear it's just the half-time whistle, it's a downer.

David Kirk mentions this in his autobiography: after Auckland had won the Ranfurly Shield with a gruelling match against Canterbury they couldn't summon the vigour to beat Otago.

When incoming governments attend their first Treasury

briefing they often have a nasty surprise. David Lange was welcomed with a currency crisis left by a vengeful outgoing Prime Minister; in return, Jim Bolger was welcomed with a bankrupt Bank of New Zealand.

The entire New Zealand First parliamentary party was rolled in their moment of victory. They had breached the citadel of Parliament; they were in the corridors of power; they were going to do great things for their people because after all the pain, strain and heartache, they had that precious jewel, that chalice that is holy to all politicians, the balance of power.

They were instantly rolled.

The Nats loved them to death. As the Maori members pointed out, it was the good manners of the Nats that captured them. "They respected us," they have said. "They told us they wanted a more Maori view of things in the government." Or they said, "Good point, Robyn!" John Delamere was most impressed with how obliging Bill Birch was. Bill Birch actually hugged Deb Morris.

And once the document was signed, the bayonet quickly and quietly undid them.

5 *Pay no attention to what politicians say: pay close attention to what they do.*

The reason I bet Owen Jennings $500 that Maurice Williamson wouldn't come and lead Act was because Williamson had done nothing someone would do if they were coming to do that peculiar thing. He had not gone through the process of leaving one party to lead another. Such a process would include making a series of speeches culminating in a speech overseas preparing the ground. You wind the media up. The principles on which you might leave are paraded and you would possess the most attractive of them and make it yours. You are attacked by your opponents in your party. The media begins to speculate about you – is this a run for power in National? Are you the long-awaited stalking horse? Or are you planning on leaving the party altogether? You announce you'll be making an announcement about your future next week. The public is now involved in the drama, you make the case, you stimulate public debate, you choose the moment, and then you arrive – applause, recrimination, it's a launch!

None of this he had done, though in private he couldn't have said more.

On a more serious plane, Muldoon said one thing and did quite the opposite. His extensive vocabulary was that of the right: hard-nosed rhetoric about the need for belt-tightening. And yet he spent money like a socialist. He began from a National position, but gradually occupied all the Labour positions as well. He was a socialist in nationalist clothing (national socialism is a concept with unfortunate historical echoes). To that extent he represented the worst of both worlds.

But many politicians still see Muldoon's position as the political centre. The argument grips them powerfully – so much so that they're still doing it. They talk privatisation, reform, fiscal discipline: very little has been reformed and the last eighteen months have been characterised by slippage. Muldoon used charisma to distract attention from the reality; Bill Birch uses a different technique: it's hard to fight Bill and take him down in a death roll when you're always nodding off.

John Banks as we have seen based his fractured career on this principle, supporting one thing in principle and another in practice, and so has Winston. (How astonished he must have been when his $100 million offer to subsidise exporters was turned down.)

And while it doesn't matter much what John Banks does any

more, or what Winston thinks for that matter, Jenny Shipley is rather a different fish. She wants to be prime minister; there are those who think she'll do it. She has a reputation as a right-winger because those are the noises she makes. But what has she done? Her reputation was formed in Social Welfare where she implemented Ruth Richardson's policy and since then has done little of consequence other than position herself as a pragmatist.

Similarly, there was a minister called Bruce Cliffe who was flirting with the idea of coming to lead Act; he was said to be absolutely on-side with policy and philosophy, was wanting to break down state monopolies. But what had this Minister of the Accident Compensation Corporation done to reform it? The organisation embodies everything that is wrong with a public policy structure (answer: zip).

Bill Birch talks like a convert to the one true way of fiscal rectitude – but he authorised the spending of billions in the run-up to the election.

6 *The correct administration of paranoia is among the first talents of politics.*

When you are running a scandal you will have material to damage your target. Two schools of thought contend. One says, "If you've got some muck – chuck it." (Old Arthur Faulkner said he had the wood on Keith Holyoake: "When I drop this," he said for twenty years, "he'll be history." – he took whatever wood it was to his own grave.) Drop the wood. Give it everything. Someone will very likely hand you some more to chuck if the first lot makes a splash.

Another school of thought recommends chucking only half. Then, when they think you're reloading and they're coming in to counter-attack, give them the real stuff.

This requires you to have the real stuff, of course.

It is essential not to let all your crackers off at once. A one-day story is a waste of effort – it's come and gone before the public have had a chance to get involved in the story, to take sides, to relish the denouement.

At the outset of a scandal do not reveal names or evidence, merely that the scandal exists and the broad bones of the story; let journalists know the evidence will be forthcoming. If they ask to see it, on no account let them do so. They will go straight to the primary sources and cut you out of the story.

At the start of the affair, give the broad outline of the scandal but don't name any participants. The media must be interested enough to speculate who the perpetrator is.

A smoking gun helps. If Jonathan Hunt had been named at the outset of the taxi chits story, it would have been a one-day wonder. It was announced the scandal of massive taxi spending existed and that someone was spending $30,000 a year. The question was: Who's the Wastrel?

This is a rule of media that Winston discovered. It expands the popular imagination. You might even say: "I am allowing them the opportunity to come forward." Sometimes, people will believe anything.

7 *The effective disbursement of public money has nothing to do with commercial reality.*

Think Big was correctly identified by National politicians as great election politics. It dramatised Muldoon as a great patriot; it promised self-sufficiency for New Zealand (we don't need those snooty foreigners any more), and it was an inspirational mission for a homely country to take up a vast technological project. Commercially of course, it was a dog. The Clyde dam was valued recently for a fraction of its cost and Fletcher's paid a dollar for a heavily endebted methanol plant.

Looking down the other end of the telescope, the dockworkers' redundancy claim – they wanted a year and a half's pay to go away – so inflamed their political masters that they refused to make the payments even though it produced a return within eighteen months. If treated as a return on capital nothing else approached it. Yet political administrations couldn't bring themselves to enrich their ancient enemies.

8 *Never seek the leadership: it is bestowed upon you.*
Jenny Shipley made a stunningly frank statement to the press this year: "I support the Prime Minister as long as he has the numbers to defeat me, but as soon as I know I can beat him I will," she said. She phrased it a little more tactfully, it must be said: "The Prime Minister has my support as long as he has the support of caucus," were her actual words.

The leadership challenge has been disabled by the lack of a stalking horse. This hapless creature goes out to challenge the leader without the least chance of winning. The horse knows this; it is the only chance at appearing in the history books. Once the challenge is made then the real contenders say, "I wouldn't for the world have thought of standing for the leadership myself. As everyone knows, loyalty is my first quality, but as an election is inevitable, I feel it is my duty to try and ensure the continuation of the tradition of governance that . . . . " (you've got the idea).

It was thought to be just possible that Lockwood was volunteering for this role earlier in the year, but that was incredible. Why wouldn't he want the job himself?

9 *When politicians say 'never', they mean 'soon'.*
We will never privatise Telecom. We will never allow advertising on television on Sundays. We will never . . . say never again.

10 *You can never kill a politician. They only commit suicide.* Winston is at three per cent; people have written him off. He's been down there before and has risen again. He will of course be taken seriously as long as he says that he is serious.

Remember how hard it was to get rid of Muldoon; the cartoons of him rearing up, cloaked and fanged from the tomb?

Michael Laws got into serious trouble with the Antoinette Beck affair (a research project for a local council was deceitfully put together and signed with a false name).

While they're up there swinging and saying they're alive, they're alive.

At the hot pools at Rotoiti only a couple of years ago there was a paper pinned up with the names of the committee.

At the bottom of the list was J.B. Leary (deceased). That is real power of personality, to still have a presence on a committee in that condition.

11 *Never tell anyone anything unless you want everyone to know.* This rule was formulated by a doyenne of Hawke's Bay social life. And it's a sad rule, it seems to me, because if you obey it you can't have any close friends.

12 *"In the first-among-equals racket, journalists are first, okay? (Jane's First Law of Journalism)*

Senior journalists – in this country, television journalists – see themselves as part of the establishment of power. It's the same everywhere. When my thirty-five-year-old friends started the *Independent* in London they instinctively chose the same level of company cars that cabinet ministers drove.

This important law was first discerned when a radio journalist told me that she'd just come back from giving Paul Keating a snaky item on the news. "I always do that to him," she told me. I wondered why. "Fifteen years ago, at my first-ever press conference, I asked Paul Keating a question and he was rude to me, so I've never given him a good report from that day to this."

Brian Edwards would agree with this. He is open about his aversion to criticism. When someone says something uncomplimentary about him in a newspaper he says he wants to kill them. His reaction is extreme and may be fortified by the fact that he never reads: personal abuse brought to his attention by well-wishers may be the only printed matter he ever absorbs.

When the economist Gareth Morgan says something admiring about Rodney Hide, this law will be subject to revision. Gareth is a voice from the right, broadly speaking, but following an exchange of letters with Rodney, he launched into a passionate, three-part attack on Act and its policies in the National Business Review. He still is fairly down in the mouth about it ("reduced to the level of perk-busting" was a recent aside in his column).

But politicians are, I think, less like this than journalists. Where journalists, like many literary people hold grudges, politicians often don't, surprising as that seems. Feathers fly, terrible things may be said – but they can the next beat be poring over technicalities of a piece of legislative drafting like colleagues. Of course, they often do hold grudges too, and this adds to the gaiety of the nation.

13 *The first victory is choosing the ground to fight on.*

In the Tuku scandal, Winston defined as acceptable anything that wasn't criminal. In any of his scandals he always changes the ground – almost at will, so good is he at it. He was attacking companies, then attacking the Serious Fraud Office, then the competence of judges. The trouble with shifting the ground is that eventually *everyone* is guilty.

14 *The first requirement for large change is speed over the ice.* Roger Douglas is shockingly frank in his speech to the Mt Pelerin Society about how to achieve structural change. Among the insights that Bevan Burgess formulated for the speech there are the following:

- Do not try to advance a step at a time. Define your objectives clearly and move towards them in quantum leaps: otherwise the interest groups will have time to mobilise and drag you down.
- Speed is essential. It is almost impossible to go too fast... Vested interests seeking to preserve past privileges will always argue strongly for a slower pace of change. Many demands for a slower pace of change are actually expressing resentment that the government is not moving fast enough to abolish privileges enjoyed by other groups.
- Once the programme begins to be implemented don't stop until you have implemented it. The fire of opponents is much less accurate if they have to shoot at a moving target.

15 *The law of opposites: when you say the opposite of what you mean, you are half- way home.*

This law of opposites operates in all areas of human experience and points to a fundamental perversity in human nature. For instance, there have been times in a relationship when I've wanted to stay in at night and *therefore* have suggested we go out.

A child complains about their shoulder hurting. After suitable expressions of sympathy we say, "Tell me if it gets any worse and we'll go and see the doctor." The pain starts to disappear almost immediately.

Act sent out a newsletter attacking Jenny Shipley for not being right-wing enough. Nothing Act could have said would have helped her more to reposition herself as a moderate.

You are in the hot pools in winter. The best way to avoid catching a cold in winter is to do the opposite of what seems sensible – jump in the cold lake (it revs your heart rate up).

In London, where there is quite a strong code of driving manners, a car starts pulling out in front of you; your initial reaction is to aim more for the centre of the road – this encourages the car to keep on coming. To stop it proceeding, you jink in towards the vehicle and it stops very abruptly.

Friends, Romans, countrymen, lend me your ears.
I come to bury Caesar, not to praise him. *(yeah, really)*
The evil that men do lives after them;
The good is oft interred with their bones;
So let it be with Caesar. The noble Brutus *(that bastard)*
Hath told you Caesar was ambitious.
If it were so, it was a grievous fault,
And grievously hath Caesar answered it.
Here, under leave of Brutus and the rest -
For Brutus is an honourable man; *(sorry, a complete bastard)*
So are they all, all honourable men - *(utter swine)*
Come I to speak in Caesar's funeral.
He was my friend, faithful and just to me;
But Brutus says he was ambitious, *(lying scum)*
And Brutus is an honourable man. *(bastard)*
He hath brought many captives home to Rome,
Whose ransoms did the general coffers fill.
Did this in Caesar seem ambitious? *(yeah, right!)*

When that the poor have cried, Caesar hath wept;
Ambition should be made of sterner stuff.
Yet Brutus says he was ambitious,
And Brutus is an honourable man. *(getting the idea about the scumbag?)*
You all did see that on the Lupercal
I thrice presented him a kingly crown,
Which he did thrice refuse. Was this ambition? *(like fun it was!)*
Yet Brutus says he was ambitious,
And sure he is an honourable man. *(so's my butt)*
I speak not to disprove what Brutus spoke, *(believe me)*
But here I am to speak what I do know . . . .

Mark Antony, Julius Caesar

Attacking often creates sympathy for the attacked – especially if the attacker wins. To defeat someone, you must lead them gently, in friendly fashion, to suicide. This is nicely illustrated by an exchange where the participants mean quite the opposite of what they were saying.

"And I want to assure Mr Muldoon there will be a place for you, sir, in the new scheme of things; there will be a place for you."

"And I love you too, Mr Lange."

Lange and Muldoon in their final television debate pre-1984 election.

On the dark side of marriage, it can be taken as a rule that when you most want to be silent you should be communicating, and when you have an overpowering urge to express yourself you should probably be biting your tongue the hardest.

There's a longer version of this important rule by a

distinguished writer now long dead, alas, but out of copyright at least. The French novelist Balzac wrote a treatise on the relations between men and women called *The Physiology of Marriage*. He relates a commanding anecdote concerning the marriages of two of his friends. One was a mathematician whose wife was particularly anxious for a diamond cross to wear to an upcoming ball.

> "It is impossible," he said with a sigh: "I will prove it to you by *a+b*."
>
> "Oh! Please don't do that," she cried, blinking her eyes and nodding towards me. If only it had been algebra, my master would have understood the look: but it was as unintelligible as Chinese to him and he continued:
>
> "Look here my dear, you shall judge for yourself: we have ten thousand francs a year. The principles of general economy demand that not more than two-tenths of one's income should be put aside for rent and servants' wages. Our house and servants cost us a hundred livres. I give you twelve hundred francs for your dress. The food amounts to four thousand francs. Our children cost at least twenty-five livres. I take for myself only eight hundred francs. The laundry, wood and lighting come to about a thousand. There remains, as you see, only six hundred francs and this amount has never been enough for unforeseen expenses. Therefore: be a good girl."
>
> "I shall have to," she said, "but you'll be the only man in Paris who has not given his wife a new year's gift."
>
> The story moves to the other friend's house where the second wife is saying to her husband: "If you were nice, Alexander, you would give me that pair of earrings we saw with the diamond sprays."
>
> "Who would not be married?" cried my friend cheerfully,

taking from his pocket-book three thousand franc notes and dazzling the sparkling eyes of his wife with them. "I can no more resist the pleasure of offering them than you can resist taking them. Today is the anniversary of the day I first saw you. The diamonds may remind you of it!"

"Naughty boy!" she said with a ravishing smile.

Never shall I forget the quickness and greedy joy with which the little woman seized upon the three notes. I could not help thinking of our professor and the difference between him and this spendthrift.

The lunch went off very gaily. We were soon installed in a small, newly-decorated drawing-room, seated by a fire that warmed the fibres and made them expand as in springtime. I complimented this loving couple on the furnishing of their little snuggery.

"It is a pity it all costs so much," said my friend, "but of course the nest must be worthy of the bird! Why the deuce do you compliment me on hangings that are not yet paid for? You remind me while I am trying to digest my lunch, that I still owe two thousand francs to a beastly upholsterer."

At these words the mistress of the house appeared to make a mental inventory of the pretty boudoir; her bright face became thoughtful. Alexander took me by the arm and dragged me over to a window seat.

"Have you by any chance three thousand francs you could lend me?" he said in a low voice.

"Alexander!" cried the dear creature, interrupting her husband and running towards us, holding out the three notes, "Alexander, I see this is madness."

"What business is it of yours?" he replied, "Keep the money."

"But I am ruining you, my love! I ought to have known that

you love me far too much for me to confide my wishes to you."

"Keep it my dear, it is a good find. Why, I shall soon win it back at cards this winter."

"Cards!" she said, with a terrified look. "Alexander, take your notes! Come, I wish it!"

"No, no," replied my friend, pushing away the delicate white hand. Are you not going to Madame de —'s ball on Thursday?"

At the ball, the mathematician's wife has the diamond cross, and Alexander's wife had a simple little child's cross on a black velvet ribbon. "What, no diamond sprays?" I asked her.

"Ah!" she said, "I enjoyed them for a whole luncheon! But you see, it has ended in my converting Alexander."

"He was easily brought round!"

A triumphant look was her only answer.

I remembered this story when they published a survey featuring net government overseas debt. A survey turned up a surprise result in the early years of the decade. The public were irritated and disenchanted with Bolger, and the country refused to accept a recovery was well under way. (This was a pre-Road to Damascus experience.) Bolger's message of hope and confidence wasn't taking. And yet, a significant proportion of New Zealanders placed as a high priority the repayment of government debt. This was very mysterious. There's no benefit to ordinary people in repaying national debt – what would be the point of that? So no politician had ever referred to it.

I deduced that it was the *one thing* we had never nagged the public about. We had been haranguing them about how well the economy was doing, exports were up, productivity was up, investment was up – our hopeless mission was trying to prove by algebra that things were getting better.

The same phenomenon was happening in England at the

same time. A minister on *Question Time* was asked about the economy and he responded with a string of positive and optimistic indicators – all of which were both true and relevant (car production up, consumer confidence rising, building permits increasing) – and the audience booed him.

Balzac's conclusion about women is something successful politicians apply to electorates. He says: "Woman has a horror of being compelled to admit the truth of any particular statement. To be persuaded she must be enticed. Exact reasoning irritates, and in the long run, annihilates her. To govern her, then, one must use those means of which she so often avails herself – feeling and sentiment."

Whether or not this is true of "woman" will be a matter of debate. But it is certainly true of electorates. If it weren't, politics would be a Corinthian profession of the greatest integrity and dignity, and there'd be no need of the dark art. Because, the fact is, that when we look into the parliamentary process we see politics and politicians that have been created in our image, in the image of us the voters, and we get, clearly, but broadly speaking, very much what we deserve.

Appendix

Words go in and out of fashion: here is a brief list of what words have been popular recently, and what the speaker seeks to convey by their use.

Broadly speaking: "I have travelled all over this area of knowledge. I know there are exceptions but I've weighed things in my balance you've never heard of. My verdict is better than yours because I know more about it."

Clearly: "*Everybody* agrees with me on this."

Confused: "There is no personal animosity in my attitude to the imbecile I'm demolishing. It is easy to see where they have gone wrong. I am intellectually superior to them – and so are you, my listeners."

Cranky: "These disaffected people are bad tempered, bad mannered and subscribe to peripheral and unreliable ideas."

Curious: (means *disgraceful*): "There's no personal animosity in my remarks. I'm an amused student of human nature." Also used to impute some sinister motive: "I do find it curious that he spoke to the media before speaking to me." A more intense version is *intriguing*. "But the person who has been leaking these documents is intriguing." Intriguing means *I think it's disgusting, frankly*. See Second Law.

Extraordinary: "Worth thinking about, certainly until I've moved onto another subject. But you probably won't get the full significance because you weren't there yourself." Used of mildly unusual matters.

Naive: "I've been around far longer than the person I'm trashing, and I know more than they do about everything, actually."

Nothing new here: "It is boring and irrelevant."

Orchestrated: "Sinister. Unnatural. Bullying."

Perplexing: "A crime has probably been committed here, but I'm so honest that criminal possibilities never enter my world view. But how else to explain these facts? It's a mystery. You work it out."

Resile: "Politics is a technical business and I am a master of it and you probably aren't. This will allow me to do the opposite of what I'm saying at the moment."

Scumbag allegations: "My accuser is a scumbag." Note – scumbag allegations are almost always correct.

Trumpeting: "They obviously think they're pretty smart they have to boast about it because no-one else is doing it for them."

Venal: "I live in a superior moral and ethical universe."

Wonky: "This is such a childish idea I'm attacking that I needn't use grown-up language to describe it to you." (Same for nuts, loopy, potty, dotty, bonkers.)

Simon Carr has lived in and out of New Zealand since 1975. He has worked in journalism, advertising and publishing here and in London. He has been an actor, playwright, novelist, critic and commentator; he has various prizes, awards and bestsellers in his attic. For two years he was Jim Bolger's speech writer, and was closely involved in the launch and development of Act New Zealand.

He is single and lives in Auckland with his two sons.